The Wars of the Roses

introductions to history

Series Editor: David Birmingham,
Professor of Modern History, University of Kent at Canterbury

A series initiated by members of the School of History at the
University of Kent at Canterbury

The Wars of the Roses

Bruce Webster

First published in 1998 by UCL Press

UCL Press Limited
1 Gunpowder Square
London EC4A 3DE
UK

and

1900 Frost Road, Suite 101
Bristol
Pennsylvania 19007-1598
USA

The name of University College London (UCL) is a registered
trade mark used by UCL Press with the consent of the owner.

British Library Cataloguing-in-Publication Data
A catalogue record for this book is available from the British Library.

Library of Congress Cataloging-in-Publication Data are available

ISBN: 1-85728-493-3 PB

Typeset in Sabon and Gill Sans by
Acorn Bookwork, Salisbury, UK.
Printed and bound by T.J. International, Padstow, UK.

Contents

Acknowledgements

I have tried in the references to the text to record specific debts to the writings of others. Inevitably, there are many more of which I am scarcely aware and which I cannot attribute. I also owe an unattributable debt to UCL Press's reader, whose very helpful and thorough report has greatly improved my text. For this I am very grateful.

Like many in my generation, I was fortunate as a student to come into contact with K. B. McFarlane, under whose guidance I spent a memorable term reading the Oxford special subject on Richard II. To those who did not know Bruce McFarlane, it is hard to convey the stimulus of his teaching, let alone his courtesy and the continuing friendship which he extended so generously. Nevertheless, I think readers of this book will see the extent of his influence.

My interest in the period also owes a great deal to my former colleague in Glasgow Dr (later Professor) A. L. Brown, who persuaded me to join him for several years in teaching a special subject on the Wars of the Roses. I learned much from that experience, and from the generations of students in Glasgow, and later at Kent, with whom I have studied the period. "Teaching" is not a one-way process: you learn at least as much as you contribute, even if the interaction is so constant that you are scarcely aware that it is happening.

In the writing I have, as always, owed more than I can express to my wife, who has read and discussed what must have seemed like endless successive drafts, to my and my readers' enormous gain.

ACKNOWLEDGEMENTS

When you have been involved in a subject for so many years, it is hard to be sure that you are conveying what seems so clear to yourself. To have a patient and constructive reader always at hand is something I have found more helpful than I can possibly convey, if not, I hope, something I take for granted.

Genealogical Table

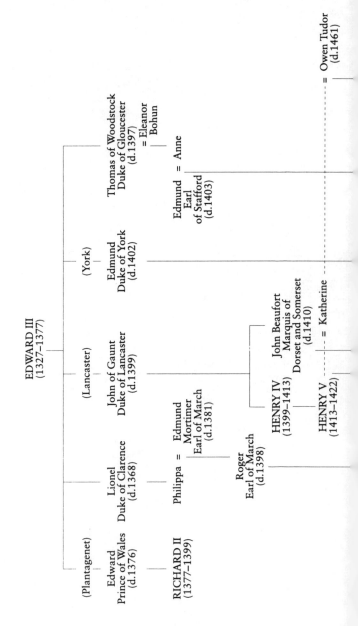

EDWARD III
(1327–1377)

(Plantagenet)

Edward
Prince of Wales
(d.1376)

RICHARD II
(1377–1399)

Lionel
Duke of Clarence
(d.1368)

Philippa = Edmund
Mortimer
Earl of March
(d.1381)

Roger
Earl of March
(d.1398)

(Lancaster)

John of Gaunt
Duke of Lancaster
(d.1399)

HENRY IV
(1399–1413)

John Beaufort
Marquis of
Dorset and Somerset
(d.1410)

HENRY V
(1413–1422)

= Katherine

(York)

Edmund
Duke of York
(d.1402)

Thomas of Woodstock
Duke of Gloucester
(d.1397)
= Eleanor
Bohun

Edmund = Anne
Earl
of Stafford
(d.1403)

= Owen Tudor
(d.1461)

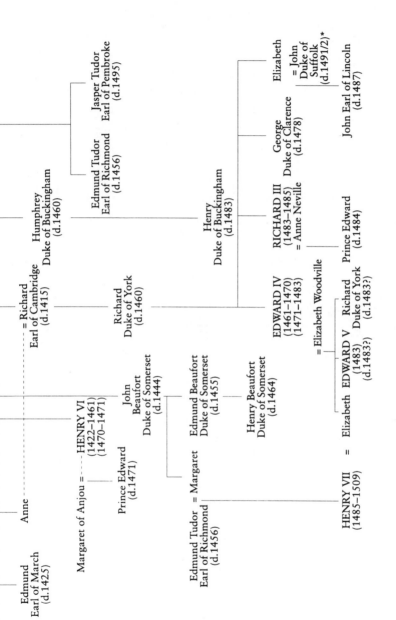

* According to The Handbook of British Chronology, John, Duke of Suffolk died between 29th October 1491 and 27th October 1492. (E. B. Fryde, D. E. Greenway, F. Porter, I. Roy, *The Handbook of British Chronology*, 3rd edn (London: Royal Historical Society, 1986).)

The Wars of the Roses

Table of Events

		Yorkist Victories	Lancastrian Victories	Other Battles etc.
1450	HENRY VI			Jack Cade's Rebellion
1452				Revolt of Duke of York
1453	Henry insane			
1454	York Protector			
1455	Henry recovered	St Albans I		
1456	York again Protector York dismissed Court removed to Coventry			Coventry Parliament
1459		Blore Heath	Ludford	
1460		Northampton	Wakefield	
1461		Mortimer's Cross	St Albans II	
1461	EDWARD IV	Towton		Berwick ceded to Scots by Henry VI
1464		Hexham		
1468		Capture of Harlech		
1469				Rebellion of Warwick and Clarence Edgecote Capture and release of

Year	Monarch	Battles	Events
1470 1471	HENRY VI	Barnet Tewkesbury	...of Warwick and Clarence Agreement with Queen Margaret Return of Warwick and Clarence
1471	EDWARD IV		Return of Edward IV Fauconberg's Rebellion
1478			Execution of Clarence
1482			Recapture of Berwick
1483	EDWARD V		
1483 1485	RICHARD III		Buckingham's Rebellion Bosworth
1485	HENRY VII		

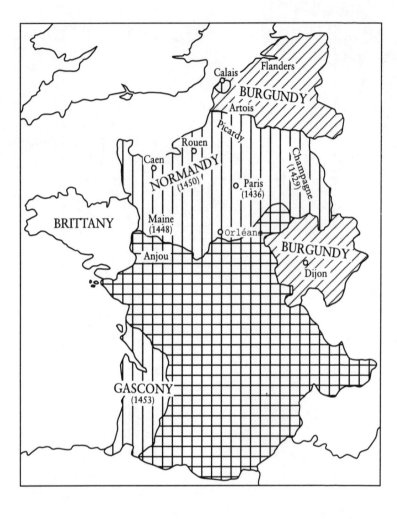

Calais

Flanders

BURGUNDY

Artois

Picardy

Rouen

Caen

NORMANDY
(1450)

Paris
(1436)

Champagne
(1429)

Maine
(1448)

Orléans

BRITTANY

Anjou

BURGUNDY

Dijon

GASCONY
(1453)

Area under English
rule in 1422

Area under Burgundian
rule in 1422

Area recognizing
Charles VII in 1422

(dates are those of recovery of provinces by French)

The Wars in France 1422–1453

The Wars of the Roses 1455–1485

CHAPTER ONE

The problem

The period from Jack Cade's rebellion in 1450 till the battle of Bosworth in 1485 has traditionally been labelled as that of the "Wars of the Roses". This conflict was allegedly between the rival houses of Lancaster and York, the descendants respectively of two sons of Edward III: John of Gaunt, Duke of Lancaster, whose son, grandson and great-grandson ruled England as Henry IV, Henry V and Henry VI from 1399 till 1461; and Edmund, Duke of York, whose remoter descendants reigned as Edward IV and Richard III from 1461, with a brief interlude in 1470–71 when Henry VI was restored, until Richard's defeat at Bosworth in 1485. There is no good evidence that anyone at the time actually referred to "The Wars of the Roses", though the Lancastrians did use a red rose as an emblem, and the Yorkists a white one; and Henry VII's "Tudor Rose" displayed both colours as a symbol of restored unity. Nevertheless, however we try to escape from it, the concept of the Wars of the Roses continues to dominate our thinking about fifteenth-century England. This is hardly surprising, for the years from 1450 to 1485 experienced a degree of political instability unparalleled since the Norman Conquest. In these 35 years, the reigning king was deposed on five occasions; and one, Henry VI, contrived to be deposed twice! Temporary breakdowns of government had occurred at other periods, even outbreaks of civil war; and in the previous century two kings, Edward II and Richard II, had actually been deposed; but such a rapid series of dynastic upheavals seems unique to the mid-fifteenth century.

In the more than 500 years which have elapsed since the Wars of the Roses, the attitude of historians towards the period has changed remarkably. For the Tudors, the explanation of the conflicts was straightforward, and it is an explanation which has influenced all later thinking. It was set forth in Tudor histories, most fully in Edward Hall's *The Union of the two noble and illustre famelies of Lancastre and Yorke* (1550), on which, largely, Raphael Holinshed based his *Chronicles*, first published in 1577. Holinshed's *Chronicles* were in turn the immediate source for Shakespeare's historical plays which eventually provided a continuous history of England from 1399 till 1485. Even to the present, it has proved very hard to escape from the influence of Shakespeare's account.

For Shakespeare, as for Tudor historians in general, the divisions of the fifteenth century went back to 1399. In their version, the deposition of Richard II established a Lancastrian dynasty which had no true right to the throne. The Wars were the eventual judgement of heaven upon the usurpers; but true peace could not be restored till the two rival dynasties were brought together and the wound of 1399 healed in the marriage of Henry VII and Elizabeth of York. This interpretation was rather elaborately set out by Edward Hall in the preface to his history, addressed to Edward VI, the young king on the throne when it was published:

> This simple treatise which I have named the Union of the noble houses of Lancaster and York, conjoined together by the godly marriage of your most noble grandfather and your virtuous grandmother [Henry VII and Elizabeth of York], for as king Henry the fourth was the beginning and root of the great discord and division; so was that godly matrimony the final end of all dissensions, titles and debates (Hall 1550: Preface).

Shakespeare's sequence of plays begins at the same point as Hall's *Union*, with the troubles at the end of Richard II's reign; and sets out the interpretation at both the start and the finish. Richard II already prophesies that his deposition will bring disasters on the country. [Richard is addressing Northumberland, who has come as messenger from Bolingbroke, the son of John of Gaunt, duke of Lancaster.]

For well we know no hand of blood and bone
Can grip the sacred handle of our sceptre
Unless he do profane, steal or usurp.
And though you think that all – as you have done –
Have torn their souls by turning them from us,
And we are barren and bereft of friends,
Yet know my master, God omnipotent,
Is mustering in his clouds on our behalf
Armies of pestilence; and they shall strike
Your children yet unborn and unbegot,
That lift your vassal hands against my head
And threat the glory of my precious crown.

(Richard II, Act 3 Sc.3, 78–89)

The end of *Richard III* records the resolution of the conflict in the closing speech of Henry of Richmond, now after his victory and the death of King Richard at Bosworth, King Henry VII:

And then – as we have ta'en the sacrament –
[This refers to his earlier promise to marry Elizabeth of York]
We will unite the white rose and the red.
Smile, heaven, upon this fair conjunction,
That long have frowned upon their enmity.
What traitor hears me and says not "Amen"?
England hath long been mad, and scarred herself;
The brother blindly shed the brother's blood;
The father rashly slaughtered his own son;
The son, compelled, been butcher to the sire;
All that divided York and Lancaster,
United in their dire division.
O now let Richmond and Elizabeth,
The true succeeders of each royal house,
By God's fair ordinance conjoin together,
And let their heirs – God, if his will be so –
Enrich the time to come with smooth-faced peace,
With smiling plenty, and fair prosperous days.

(Richard III, Act 5 Sc.8, 18–34)

3

This picture, as we shall see, bore little resemblance to what actually happened, either in the fifteenth or the sixteenth century. The first was by neither so universally violent and disordered, nor the second so peaceful, as Shakespeare suggested. But it answered very directly to the needs of the Tudor governments and the aspirations of many of their people.

The truth was that the Tudor monarchy was by no means so secure or universally trusted and admired as it liked to claim, and power was maintained by a violence, which often, as under Henry VIII, bordered on terror. The dynasty was threatened by a multiplicity of plots, especially during the reign of Elizabeth; Mary Queen of Scots, while she lived, served as a focus for dissidents, and, even more seriously, as an invitation for foreign invasion. In this intermittently charged atmosphere, the fifteenth century and particularly the period of the Wars of the Roses, provided a horrific example of the dangers of disorder and overmighty subjects, to which the only antidote was loyalty to a strong and respected monarchy.

The lesson was underlined, for instance, in successive editions of the *Mirror for magistrates* from 1559 to 1587 (Campbell 1938). It was a collection of cautionary *exempla* in verse, starting with the career of "Robert Tresilian chiefe Justice of Englande" who was executed by the "Merciless Parliament" of 1388 as one of the alleged evil advisers of Richard II, and continuing with a series of rebels, disturbers of the peace and good order, down to Richard III and beyond. Its object was to bring out the qualities of the evil politicians who threatened the order and stability of the realm and to warn magistrates, those in power and influence, against such conduct. All the *exempla* were designed to emphasize the awful consequences of disloyalty and personal ambition. The moral, the importance of submission to the crown as the only upholder of order in society, was repeated in many of the official proclamations of the day (see, for example, Campbell 1964: 214–18). The same reasoning may explain the fascination for the career of Richard III, a central figure in the *Mirror for magistrates*, and the subject of at least two other plays in the reign of Elizabeth, in addition to Shakespeare's. Richard was the ultimate example of the dreadful results of a self-seeking ambition which pursued its own advancement, reckless of the welfare of the commonwealth and every moral principle. The Wars of the Roses exemplified some of the deepest fears of Tudor governments and their subjects. Hence their prominence in Tudor histories and literature.

Shakespeare reflected these worries very explicitly in the closing lines of Richmond's speech at the end of *Richard III*, as imperceptibly the scene shifts forward from 1485 to the 1590s in which Shakespeare was writing:

> Abate the edge of traitors, gracious Lord,
> That would reduce these bloody days again
> And make poor England weep forth tears of blood.
> Let them not live to taste this land's increase,
> That would with treason wound this fair land's peace.
> Now civil wounds are stopped; peace lives again.
> That she may long live here, God say "Amen".

> (*Richard III*, Act 5 Sc.8, 35–41)

At the same time, the threat of foreign invasion, particularly on behalf of the Catholic Mary Queen of Scots, underlined the importance of loyalty to the crown. Elizabeth was not only the surety against internal disorder, but also the focus for a national defence of England against foreign dominance and Catholicism.

After 1603, the fifteenth century lost its topicality. The Stuart dynasty appeared secure, for a time at least, and the threat alike from over-mighty and ambitious nobles and of foreign invasion faded. When in the 1630s the dynasty did come under stress, the issues were very different. Opponents did indeed look to history, but in the conflicts of the 1630s and 40s, they turned to Magna Carta, the early history of parliament, and the Anglo-Saxon and Norman constitutions. The Wars of the Roses receded into the limbo of a history which had no particular relevance to contemporary struggles.

This is not to say that the Wars of the Roses were forgotten. The Tudor account had been intensely personal, a story of individual rampant barons culminating in the fiendish picture of Richard III. That was never to lose interest, and for three centuries, debate was to centre on the defence of Richard III from what some came to regard as the calumnies of the Tudors. George Buck in the seventeenth century (Buck 1646)and Horace Walpole in the eighteenth (Walpole 1768) both agreed that Richard was a capable king, traduced by Tudor propaganda. Buck claimed to produce some documentary evidence for his case, including a letter from Elizabeth of York suggesting that she was looking forward to the prospect of marrying Richard, a scheme which we know he entertained but was forced by his supporters to abandon. Unfortunately, the letter, if it ever existed, seems to be lost! Most of the arguments for Richard depended not on evidence, but on the claim that the monster of the Tudor account was impossible to believe in.

By the nineteenth century, historians were becoming more concerned with the documents, many of which had been made available by the antiquaries of the seventeenth and eighteenth centuries. The parliament rolls, the basis of any study of the workings of parliament, had been printed in the late eighteenth century. Before the end of the nineteenth century, many more records were to be published, at least in summary, in the series of calendars of public records which were then appearing. But in Victorian Britain when Parliament dominated the political scene, it was above all the history of parliament that interested historians. Bishop Stubbs' great classic, the *Constitutional history of England* (Stubbs 1874–78), was in its essentials a narrative of the growth of parliament and of its proceedings; and to that story the fifteenth century was a rather distressing appendage, a period when the hopeful developments of the thirteenth and fourteenth centuries were overtaken by what seemed a lapse into barbarism. Similarly, T. F. Tout's fundamentally new exploration of the development of royal government in his *Chapters in the administrative history of medieval England* (Tout 1920–33) stopped in 1399. This gave the impression that development here too stopped during the fifteenth century, until progress was resumed in the seemingly new developments of the Tudors. Given the masses of documents that existed, Tout had taken the story much further than would have seemed possible for one person, even aided as he was by a few devoted researchers. It was some time before the history of administration was taken very far into the thickly documented fifteenth century.

Meanwhile, the argument about Richard III continued, and as the century advanced became more thoroughly based on the documents that were becoming available. Few, however, were concerned to defend Richard. The most learned of students of the subject, James Gairdner, who was an experienced and excellent editor of documents, produced what remained till 1981 the best biography of Richard III, based on a masterly grasp of the sources (Gairdner 1898); but he, like many other historians, remained convinced that tradition provided the best guide to historical truth, and so adhered firmly to the Tudor line. Most authorities followed him. The only divergent voices of note were Caroline Halstead, whose biography of Richard III, published in 1844, went so far in the direction of adulation as to be hard to accept; and, at the end of the nineteenth century, Sir Clements Markham, a distinguished civil servant and geographer, who argued vehemently, and with a good deal of critical sense, that the sources for Richard III's reign were too prejudiced and, as he thought, too deliberately distorted, to be relied on (Markham 1891). His arguments have been taken up by defenders of Richard in the various pro-Richard III societies that have grown up in the present century. However, in his efforts to exonerate Richard from what has always been seen as his greatest crime, Markham tried to fix on Henry VII the responsibility for the murder of Edward IV's sons, the "princes in the Tower". This is just possible, because we have no good evidence at all as to what really happened to them; but it is very hard to believe that they could have survived, completely without record, in the Tower of London or elsewhere, from 1483 till after Bosworth in 1485.

These arguments did not take our understanding of the fifteenth century much further. That had to wait for two developments: first the publication in 1925 of C. L. Kingsford's Ford lectures on *Prejudice and promise in fifteenth century England* which were based on a dispassionate survey of the narrative sources for the fifteenth century by one who knew them very well; and then the lectures and writings of K. B. McFarlane who turned attention away from the *cause célèbre* towards a much wider understanding of the late medieval nobility, previously often regarded as the overmighty and violent villains of the story. McFarlane's writings, and even more his teaching, over 35 years, created a quite new attitude to the fifteenth century. He sought to place the nobles in the context of their own time, and of the circumstances of their lives, especially their dependence on landed wealth, and on maintaining a following of retainers and tenants. These topics were quite extensively illustrated in the estate documents and other records of the time. McFarlane's pupils, and others who came under his influence, went on to research the lesser landowning classes, the gentry of the fifteenth century. They proved often to be more independent, and more important for our understanding of the politics of the time than had appeared. Some of them, notably the Paston family in Norfolk, left collections of letters which give us a direct insight into their attitudes and concerns (for details on the Paston letters, see Further Reading); but many more have been the subject of the regional studies which are now essential to our understanding of what was going on.

Hence, the Wars of the Roses have come to be seen as an aspect of a landed society which needs to be studied in all its aspects. Only then can we hope to understand the problems of that society, and the causes of the breakdowns of order which occurred intermittently in the years between 1450 and the establishment of the Tudors after 1485.

There are, however, certain problems inherent in the sources which are available for this complex period. What were for long the most widely read and influential narratives, the *Anglica Historia* (English History) of Polydore Vergil (Vergil 1534) and the *History of King Richard III* by Thomas More (Sylvester 1963) were both written in the second decade of the sixteenth century, long after the battle of Bosworth in 1485 and the establishment of the Tudor dynasty. Vergil was an Italian cleric and humanist who came to England in 1502 and stayed here for most of the rest of his career. He presented a manuscript of his history to Henry VIII in 1513. It was a history of England from the earliest times, in Renaissance style, produced as an offering to the Tudor monarchy, in the hope of patronage. Even if his rewards were modest, he was apparently content, since he remained here through the upheavals of the English Reformation until he retired to his native Urbino in 1550. His history was a serious work of scholarship, based on the available sources, and showed considerable critical sense; but his account of the fifteenth century and of the Wars of the Roses in particular was inevitably written from a Tudor point of view. It was therefore unsympathetic to the Yorkists in general and particularly to Richard III. Thomas More's history is a more complex work. Drafted around the same time as Vergil was writing, it was not printed till well after More's death, and exists now in a number of different manuscript and printed versions (see Sylvester 1963). It was a vehement attack on Richard III and is the source of most of the routine Tudor and later denunciations of that king. Yet it also contains many details which have the air of being accurate reports of contemporary comments (More's father was a prominent London citizen at the time of Richard's usurpation and reign), though few of these details can be corroborated. More's account is the ultimate source for much of Shakespeare's picture of Richard III, and the source also of most subsequent hostile accounts of that king. It is also the principal target of those who wish to defend Richard III.

Much better sources for the whole period are the various continuations of the "Croyland Chronicle" (Riley, 1854; Pronay and Cox 1986; see also Gransden 1982: 265–74). These are puzzling works. The "Croyland Chronicle" itself is a fifteenth-century forgery, apparently concocted to support some legal disputes in which the abbey was involved; but the forged text was then continued, first by a narrative written by the prior of Croyland taking the story to 1469 (usually described as "The Continuation of the Croyland Chronicle") which is of considerable value for the 1460s; and then by an anonymous "Second Continuation" which corrects what it describes as some of the misconceptions of the previous author, and carries on the story to 1486. Although the "Second Continuation" does include passages about the history of the abbey which may be by a different hand, the bulk of the text appears from internal evidence to be written by someone who held official office in the Yorkist court. He was probably on the staff of Chancery or the Privy Seal Office and almost certainly played some part in diplomacy. There have been several suggested identifications, but none has yet commanded acceptance. Whoever he was, he was very well informed and, so far as can be checked, accurate. He also expresses his opinions strongly, if sometimes guardedly. This is far and away the most reliable guide to the period from the mid 1460s till 1485. A note at the end of the text says that it was completed in ten days at Croyland in April 1486, though it is not clear whether this refers to the whole text, or only to part of it. Otherwise, there is no indication of how this civil servant came to be writing a continuation to a Croyland Chronicle.

There are also a considerable number of other narratives, many of which were being written more or less contemporaneously with events, and often contain very useful information; but their value at any point depends on the knowledge of their authors. They often have particular local insights, but in assessing them we need to be alert to the point of view of the writers, and to the limitations of their sources.

These narratives are broadly of two types, both commonly, though not always, written in English. First there are continuations of the English histories which go back to the origins of Britain. These are generally called "Bruts" because, in them, British origins go back to the Trojan Brutus who was supposed to have settled in Britain, and from whom the Britons were allegedly descended. These stories are derived from Geoffrey of Monmouth's "History of the Britons", written in the 1130s (Thorpe 1966); but many versions were continued and brought up to date, and some can provide very helpful insights into contemporary events. Such was the *English chronicle of the reigns of Richard II, Henry IV, Henry V and Henry VI* (Davies 1856), which contains particularly useful information, written from a southern English point of view, on events in the later 1450s.

The second main type of contemporary chronicle is the town chronicle, chiefly and most usefully the London chronicles, which regularly provide first class information. Especially useful are the various short London chronicles. At the end of the century, these were developed into larger London chronicles, probably by Robert Fabyan, who died in 1513. However, his versions have the disadvantage of hindsight, being put together under the Tudors. For contemporary insights, one has to look at the more scattered and often scrappy earlier chronicles. (For an account of these, see Gransden 1982: Chapter 8.)

In addition to these, there are a number of important narratives which do not quite fit these categories. One is the chronicle attributed to John Warkworth, master of Peterhouse College, Cambridge, now existing as an addition to a manuscript of Caxton's "Chronicles of England" (itself a version of the "Brut"). This contains some sharp comments on the attitudes of the 1460s, though its chronology is at times confused. There are also two "official" but very detailed narratives, the *Chronicle of the rebellion in Lincoln-*

shire, 1470, and the *History of the arrival in England of Edward IV and the final recovery of his kingdoms from Henry VI, 1471.* These last were both composed by officials (unnamed) of Edward IV and were propaganda accounts of his victories, though the *Arrival* in particular has many very penetrating insights into what lay behind the events. (All three are reprinted in Dockray 1988. For a discussion see Gransden 1982: 257–65.)

Finally, since it was only printed for the first time in 1936, there is the intriguing *Usurpation of Richard III* by another Italian humanist, Dominic Mancini, who visited London between 1482 and July 1483. It was composed for Angelo Cato, Archbishop of Vienne in the south of France, as an essay which aimed to describe how Richard seized the throne (Armstrong 1969; discussion in Gransden 1982: 300–7). Since we are told in the conclusion that it was completed in December 1483, it is strictly contemporary; and is a priceless account of opinions and attitudes of the time. In using it, however, one has to remember that Mancini was dependent on what he was told and could observe. Some of his background information may well derive from Ricardian propaganda being put about in May and June during the machinations that led to the usurpation. This should not necessarily be regarded as an accurate account of past events! Although some of this material is apparently sympathetic to Richard III, it is noticeable that Mancini's account of the usurpation itself is distinctly anti-Richard. He sees the usurpation very much as a coup carried through by terror.

We also have a very large number of personal letters of gentry families, above all of the Pastons (Gairdner 1904, Davis 1971–6), but also of the Stonors, and the Cely and Plumpton families. This is something which exists for no earlier period in England. Earlier letter collections were deliberately compiled on classical models as literary exercises; these letters are genuine personal, business and sometimes political letters. They give us an insight into local affairs, especially the concerns of the Pastons in East Anglia, and an understanding of the attitudes of the gentry which can hardly be acquired from other sources.

There is also, in the records of fifteenth century courts, a mass of legal documentation about estate affairs, and sometimes the personal quarrels of the landed classes. These are not easily accessible, but have recently been much used in detailed studies of particular areas, such as Wright 1983 on Derbyshire, and Carpenter 1992 on Warwickshire. As we shall see, the gentry in the localities played a very important part in the politics of the age, yet it is a part which is easily overlooked in the general narratives. These detailed studies, and the complex evidence on which they are based, let us understand much more fully what the local gentry were really concerned about – primarily their lands and fortunes, family marriages, and litigation over their estates – rather than the high matters of dynastic conflicts which dominate our picture of the period. They were far more concerned with getting on with whomsoever had the authority to influence their personal welfare.

None of these sources will in themselves provide a ready-made answer to the principal question that now concerns historians of the period. Why was the mid-fifteenth century such a disturbed and traumatic time? From Tudor times to the present writers have sought for an answer. Could the aftermath of the Hundred Years' War, which ended disastrously for England in the early 1450s, provide an explanation? Failure clearly aroused resentment against those who seemed responsible. Moreover, after long wars in France, it was perhaps easy to transfer to England the lawless violence which was usually tolerated on campaigns abroad. Did this explain the readiness of the aggrieved to take up arms?

Some historians have pointed to specific economic problems, particularly the disruption of trade in the 1450s and a collapse of wool exports, causing considerable economic hardship to previously prosperous sheep-farmers and merchants whose wealth had depended on the wool trade. At other periods, economic troubles have sometimes coincided with periods of political instability, though in this case the exact connection is not easy to see.

Beyond this, there were wider social changes which might have helped to destabilize the political community in the mid-fifteenth century. The relations of landlords and tenants had changed in the century after the onset of the Black Death and the fall in population which resulted. The dearth of tenants made it more difficult for the lords to enforce their rights to labour–services, and so to farm their estates. Attempts in the 1350s to re-enforce services were soon abandoned, and in the years after the Great Revolt of 1381, serfdom and villeinage quietly disappeared in favour of money rents. This not only deprived lords of some of their direct authority over their tenants; it also opened up a market in rented lands which were in effect free of the traditional burdens. Hence the possibility of some of these former peasants rising to the status of landholders of some consequence: to become "yeomen", in the language of the late fourteenth century, and even, in the fifteenth century, to join those known to historians as the gentry. These changes helped to confirm the position of the gentry as independent landholders and as a political force at no-one's beck or call. The nobility had lost something of their automatic power. They now had to depend far more on managing their "retainers", themselves men of some substance, who had chosen in their own interest to attach themselves to great nobles. This was a bond which could be broken if it ceased to be in the interests of the retainer. Hence the development of what has been dismissively called "bastard feudalism", a system which has been regarded as inherently unstable, since loyalties could easily shift and decay. Fifteenth-century nobles may have sensed that their authority was fragile, and been the more aggressive as a result.

A more immediate and specific cause of trouble in the 1450s was the collapse of royal finances which were, apparently, in a worse state by the end of the 1440s than at any other period for which we have evidence. This was one point made by Jack Cade and his fellow rebels in complaints against the mismanagement and incompetence of Henry VI's courtiers. As they put it, "himself [Henry VI] so poor that he may not pay for his meat nor drink; he oweth more than ever did king in England" (Harvey 1991: 189).

All these changes are part of the background to the troubles of the years from 1450 to 1485. They point to factors which could have contributed to a fraught situation, and we shall have to consider them more closely later; but do they quite explain the recurrent troubles which beset not just Henry VI but Edward IV and Richard III after him? We naturally seek rationally satisfying causes which lie deeper than mere immediate contingencies. Yet the Wars of the Roses were above all political events; and in the end, politics may provide a more comprehensible explanation of what happened than any of the more deep-seated factors which existed in the background.

Medieval politics had always been punctuated by occasional episodes of violent revolt. There was no mechanism in medieval political structures by which protests could be made effective, no way in which powerful discontented subjects could express their grievances effectively except by revolt. The more successful medieval kings, William the Conqueror, Henry II, Edward I, Edward III, Henry V, took the trouble to carry their nobles with them, to avoid arousing hostility by acts of injustice or excessive favouritism; thus Edward I and Edward III could on occasion listen to protests and conciliate discontent. But if kings did not, there was no way short of revolt to make them. As we shall see later, the typical baronial revolt was a protest movement, an attempt to bring pressure on the ruler to change his ways; it was not, usually, an attempt to remove the king, unless he proved, like Edward II "incorrigible without hope of amendment" (Chrimes and Brown 1961: 37–8). Revolt was a comparatively regular aspect of medieval political debate. It is therefore not surprising that discontent at Henry VI's incompetence and favouritism should have provoked rebellions at various levels in society, from the commons of Kent to some of the greatest nobles in the land.

What is unusual in the mid-fifteenth century is that revolt should have recurred so frequently; and that it should so often have resulted in the removal of the king and his replacement by a rival. It is to this in particular that we must attend in trying to explain the Wars of the Roses.

We must also remember that in the Wars of the Roses accident and contingency played a large part in determining the outcome, especially since a relatively small proportion of the population was involved. Battles such as Towton (1461) and Bosworth (1485) seem so decisive that we are apt to assume that they were the result of deep-seated factors which must have lain behind the respective victories of Edward IV and Henry VII. Yet the Lancastrians who lost Towton had, only three months before, won the apparently equally decisive battle of Wakefield (1460), and Henry VII had seemed on the brink of defeat only the night before Bosworth. The chances of the day had a profound effect: had Henry been the one to be killed at Bosworth, we might hardly have heard of the Tudors! As we shall see in the narrative which follows in Chapter 2, there were many other moments when accidents played an important part. We should not assume that what actually happened was inevitable.

Before we can take up the analytical questions which are our main concern, we must first establish, at least in outline, the course of events in what proved to be a singularly complex period. To this we must now turn.

The events: What actually happened?

Shakespeare's plays have not only confused our understanding of the fifteenth century by canonizing the interpretations current in the Tudor period; they have also misled us seriously over what actually happened. A play compresses into a few hours events that occurred over many years, and a playwright inevitably foreshortens and simplifies, in order to fit his dramatic purposes. Events in real life do not happen as they do on a stage. The fifteenth century was a very complex period, and the crises were at times bewildering in the speed and extent of the reversals of fortune. It is easy to despair of ever making sense of what was going on. We shall begin with the background to the outbreak of open war in 1455.

The war in France

What is known as the Hundred Years' War began in 1337 when Edward III announced his intention to pursue his claim to the French throne, a claim which derived from his mother Isabella, the daughter of Philip IV of France. Under Edward III himself, king of England from 1327 to 1377, and Henry V (1413–22) there had been notable victories (Crécy 1346, Poitiers 1356, Agincourt 1415) but there had also been long periods of frustrating attrition, when campaigns achieved little and territory was gradually recovered by the French. With hindsight it may seem obvious that the conquest of France was beyond England's strength; yet in 1420 Henry V had achieved the treaty of Troyes, by which he was accepted as the heir to the elderly and insane Charles VI of France, and married Charles's daughter Katherine.

This apparent triumph owed more to divisions within the French kingdom than to the strength of Henry's position. After the battle of Agincourt, in 1415, Henry had laboriously managed to conquer Normandy and Maine; but much of the rest of the country recognized the Dauphin Charles, son of Charles VI (see Map: The Wars in France, p. xiv); Henry's success in 1420 depended heavily on support from the duke of Burgundy, Philip the Good, who had been alienated from France by the treacherous murder of his father, John the Fearless, in 1419. If the conquest of France was to be a reality, there was still much to do; but Henry died in 1422, leaving his kingdom to his 9-month-old son, Henry VI. During Henry's minority, England was to be governed by a council headed by his uncles, the dukes of Bedford (died 1435) and Gloucester (died 1447) and the bishop of Winchester, Cardinal Beaufort (died 1447). The council's task would in any case have been hard; it was made much more difficult by frequent quarrels between these three leaders. The late 1420s saw an increasingly effective recovery of France, inspired by Joan of Arc and under the leadership of the Dauphin, who was more and more accepted as the lawful ruler of France, Charles VII. In 1435, after an abortive Peace Conference at Arras, Philip the Good reverted to the French allegiance, and English prospects of victory in the war became very slim.

The personal rule of Henry VI, 1437–1450

Henry VI assumed personal control in 1437, just before his sixteenth birthday. He was the grandson of Henry IV who had deposed Richard II in 1399 and had established what has come to be known as the Lancastrian dynasty, named after Henry IV's father, John of Gaunt, duke of Lancaster (see Genealogical Table, pp. x–xi). Not surprisingly, he was anxious to assert his authority and there is much evidence of his personal initiatives, both in the management of government and in foreign affairs. Yet he entered on a difficult inheritance. Despite the setback at the Congress of Arras, the war continued. Much effort was still being devoted to the defence of Calais: even as Henry assumed personal control, the town was threatened by a planned Burgundian attack on nearby Guisnes. Normandy also was being strongly held, but Gascony in the south-west of France was increasingly left to its own devices. Henry himself was temperamentally inclined to seek peace. He was strongly religious and evidently disliked war. He may also have been affected by the thought that his mother was French, though Katharine herself had little if any contact with him and died, after a long illness, in 1437. Henry however showed conspicuous favour to her second husband, Owen Tudor and their children, Edmund and Jasper, who were created respectively earls of Richmond and Pembroke in 1452. Yet his policy was supported, at least initially, by many who had recent experience of the war and recognized its hopelessness. Unfortunately, whatever the merits of the policy in itself, its execution proved disastrous.

To achieve peace he sought a French marriage and was ready to give up the territory of Maine, which had been gained by Henry V in the years after Agincourt. In the process, Henry was out-manoeuvred by the astute Charles VII of France, and got little in return for his concessions beyond marriage to Margaret of Anjou, the poorly endowed daughter of Charles VII's brother-in-law, René count of Anjou and titular king of Naples. The marriage took place in 1445. The cession of Maine was enforced by Charles VII in a campaign in 1448.

Unfortunately, the idea of peace was anathema to many, headed by the duke of Gloucester, who remained wedded to the vision of victory, the most pernicious of the legacies left by Henry V. Gloucester was naturally supported by those who were becoming desperate to hold on to the gains of land and positions in France which they had made in the years of success. This opened a serious rift among the leading English nobles, and it would have taken a very able king to achieve either victory or an effective peace in such a fraught situation.

At home, Henry was over-generous to his servants, and built up a household circle headed by William de la Pole, ultimately duke of Suffolk, which he made little attempt to control. Court servants were able to use their influence to gain positions and profit for themselves and their friends. This aroused widespread resentment at all levels in society. There was also resentment among certain nobles, such as the duke of York, who felt that they were being excluded from the power which was being abused by Suffolk and his friends. There is a surprising number of cases in the 1440s of quite ordinary people being prosecuted for speaking ill of the king, often in quite outspoken terms.

The attack on Henry VI, 1450–56

Henry's peace initiative collapsed in the late 1440s and discontent erupted into revolt. The French were now attacking Normandy; in desperation and in the hope of essential supply, a Parliament was called in November 1449, which was prorogued till January 1450. When it reassembled, there was still no grant; even a third session in May offered only very limited taxes on very restrictive conditions. Instead, in January, Suffolk was impeached, being blamed both for failure in France and corruption at home. Henry tried to save him by sending him into exile, but Suffolk was seized and murdered on the way, and a whole series of rebellions broke out in the summer of 1450. The most important, in Kent, was led by a certain Jack Cade. He and his followers managed to hold London for a few days and succeeded in executing a number of the court circle who were particularly unpopular in Kent.

This revolt also provided an opportunity for the duke of York, then lieutenant in Ireland, to return to England. He had inherited a claim to the throne through the marriage of his father to Anne, daughter of Roger earl of March (d. 1398) (see Genealogical Table, pp. x–xi). Leaving his post in Ireland without permission, he landed in North Wales, and claimed that it was his right, in this emergency, to restore order and good government. At a parliament in the autumn of 1450, he emerged as a leader of opposition to the apparently discredited court group. His retainer, Sir William Oldhall, was chosen as Speaker. Yet in the longer run York achieved little. An attempt to have him declared heir presumptive was immediately rebuffed by Henry, although Henry himself was still without a direct heir after five years of marriage. It was the first time that York, in this case through a supporter who made the proposal, had openly referred to his possible claim to the throne, and the proposal had been swept aside. By the end of the parliament, in the early summer of 1451, Henry had in effect recovered his authority after the humiliations of the first half of 1450, and many of Suffolk's friends retained their influence under the duke of Somerset, who had replaced Suffolk as Henry's principal counsellor.

York was clearly frustrated; and early in 1452, he raised an army in a further effort to remove Somerset. The attempt was a futile failure. Henry, with new-found energy, produced a much larger army at Blackheath to confront York's force at Dartford, and York had to submit. Somerset remained at liberty and in the king's confidence.

After this humiliation, York withdrew from politics, and only emerged as a result of the irretrievable loss of Gascony, after the defeat and death of John Talbot, Earl of Shrewsbury, at Castillon in July 1453. The news of this disaster apparently led to the onset of Henry's madness. The exact nature of the illness has been much disputed; possibly it was catatonic schizophrenia. Whatever it was, Henry was totally unresponsive to everyone and everything. This rapidly paralysed government; in the early months of 1454 York was appointed as Protector. The rivalry between York and Somerset was now the chief factor in politics, round which there coalesced a number of other quarrels, particularly between individuals in the many branched Neville family and the almost equally complex family of the Percies, earls of Northumberland.

For the moment, York was supreme; but his power depended on Henry's madness, which proved only a temporary breakdown. By early in 1455, the king had apparently recovered, though he never wholly regained the energy which he had displayed in 1452–3; and York's protectorate came to an end. Thereafter Henry fell increasingly under the influence of his young queen, Margaret of Anjou, whose assertiveness had been increased by the birth of a son, Prince Edward, in October 1453. Thereafter she was determined at all costs to uphold his interests, to which end she had unsuccessfully tried to be made regent in 1454.

The consequence was that York and those who now supported him, notably the Neville earl of Salisbury and his son the earl of Warwick, resorted to open rebellion. They proclaimed their loyalty to Henry, but demanded the dismissal of Somerset, who still retained Henry's confidence. This they achieved in the first battle of St Albans, on 22 May 1455, in which Henry himself was accidentally wounded (he took no part in the fighting) and Somerset was killed. This placed Henry in the control of York and his allies. Thus when Henry suffered a further attack of mental illness in November 1455, York was once again briefly established as Protector.

The Lancastrian recovery? 1456-59

In the spring of 1456, Henry was able at least nominally to resume authority. Since he rarely asserted himself, power rested increasingly with the queen, though York was, for the moment, given the important task of defending the north against a planned Scottish invasion, a threat which in the autumn resulted only in a brief Scottish raid into Northumberland.

In the summer of 1456, Margaret removed the court to Coventry, where it was surrounded by lands held by the Lancastrian crown and its supporters, and established her servants in virtually all the offices of government. By the autumn, when Henry joined his queen in Coventry, York and his principal supporters, the Neville earls of Salisbury and Warwick, were excluded from government and ceased almost entirely to attend such Great Councils as were called.

York himself was still lieutenant in Ireland. Warwick had been granted the captaincy of Calais after the battle of St Albans, though he was not able to take up the office till York became Protector. Once there, however, he was able to hold on to the position, despite several efforts by the queen's supporters to dislodge him. These external positions, especially the foreign contacts which Warwick developed from Calais, were to be very important. Moreover, Queen Margaret's assertiveness aroused a degree of hostility which could be an asset to York and his friends. Nevertheless, York, Salisbury and Warwick were isolated, with few open supporters, and increasingly afraid that the queen planned to destroy them. The king himself seems to have tried reconciliation, arranging the futile "loveday" at St Paul's in January 1458 in which the hostile groups made a show of friendship; but it meant nothing. By the end of the year, York and his friends, anxious to prevent an onslaught from the queen, raised their forces.

The conflict which followed was curiously indecisive. In September 1459, Salisbury, on the way from his castle of Middleham in Yorkshire to join Warwick and York on the marches of Wales, routed a larger Lancastrian army at Blore Heath in Staffordshire;

but in October in a battle at Ludford in Shropshire, some of Warwick's garrison from Calais, who had accompanied him to England, deserted to the royal side, and the Yorkist leaders abandoned the field and escaped to their overseas bases: York to Ireland; Warwick, Salisbury and York's son, the earl of March, the future Edward IV, to Calais. Margaret was then able, in a parliament at Coventry in November 1459, to attaint them of treason and declare all their lands forfeit; but they remained at liberty and Margaret's apparent triumph was to prove as hollow as the loveday in the previous year. York was out of reach; and attempts to recover control of Calais came to nothing.

The triumph of York

The exiled and attainted earls had in fact many advantages. They were greatly helped by Margaret's unpopularity. The withdrawal of the court to the Midlands had alienated those in London and the south-east who had profited greatly from the business which flowed from the king, his courtiers and officials while they were in London. Rumours were rife, too, of the hostile intentions of courtiers towards areas which they might suspect of supporting Warwick. Moreover, Warwick, an experienced sea commander with a small personal fleet which he had built up in Calais, was more or less in control of the Channel, and therefore could make contact with York in Ireland.

From Calais, Warwick was also able to send raids to Sandwich in January 1460, when the Lancastrian commanders at the port were humiliatingly captured, and again in June when a bridgehead was established as a base for a full invasion led by Warwick, Salisbury and March. Large numbers of Kentishmen joined their force, which was readily admitted into London, only the Tower holding out; and the main party, led by Warwick and March, passed on speedily to encounter and defeat the king's army at Northampton on 10 July.

Queen Margaret, with her young son Prince Edward, and many of her leading supporters escaped, but Henry was captured, and led back to London, with every sign of respect from Warwick and March. The impression given was that their intention was simply to take control of the king, after removing his "evil counsellors", and set up their own government in his name. To this end, apparently, a parliament was summoned to meet at Westminster on 7 October 1460. So far, York himself had remained in Ireland, from which he only returned in early September; and when he did, his actions suggest that he was already determined to claim the crown. He adopted the arms of England undifferenced, instead of those he had previously used as a descendant of Edward III. When he appeared in parliament on 10 October he attempted to take the king's place on the throne.

This was certainly unexpected and unwelcome to the majority, even of the anti-Lancastrian nobility present at the parliament. It produced an impasse, which was only, and awkwardly, resolved at the end of the month when Henry agreed that York should replace his son, Prince Edward, as heir to the throne. This led directly to war, for Margaret and her supporters could never accept it and were at liberty and preparing to fight. They had substantial support in the north and west of the country, and their troops assembled rapidly.

York and his supporters had to take the field, though it was probably unwise to seek battle in the north where support for the Lancastrians was strong, and their own army heavily outnumbered. York and Salisbury were surprised and routed at Wakefield on 30 December 1460; York was killed, and Salisbury was executed by mob violence after the battle. Warwick, who until then had remained in London with Henry VI, now took his royal prisoner with such troops as he could assemble to confront the queen's forces which were now making for the capital. At the second battle of St Albans, on 17 February 1461, Warwick's attempt failed. He and the other surviving Yorkists fled the field, leaving Henry to rejoin his wife.

At this point, Margaret might have been expected to press on to London, which was near at hand. The citizens expected her imminent arrival and feared they would be plundered by her, mainly northern, forces. There has never been any satisfactory explanation of why she did not enter the capital. For whatever reason, she and her army withdrew to the north. Even contemporary commentators realised that this was a crucial act.

Meantime, York's son, Edward earl of March, had gone west to deal with Lancastrian forces being assembled on the Welsh marches by Jasper Tudor, Henry's half-brother and earl of Pembroke since 1452 or 1453. Edward won a decisive victory at Mortimer's Cross in Herefordshire, around 2 February. Around 19 February, two days after Warwick's defeat at St Albans, Edward set out for London. Warwick, with the remains of his army, joined him on the way, and they reached the capital on 26 February, where Edward was welcomed as a saviour after the terror aroused in the city by the threat from Margaret's army.

Edward's aims were clear cut: he seized the throne in carefully stage-managed ceremonies on 3 and 4 March; and at once raised an army to deal with Margaret's troops. In less than a fortnight, he set out for the north, and on 29 March met the Lancastrian forces at Towton, near Ferrybridge. It was the largest and bloodiest battle in the Wars of the Roses, an absolute and decisive victory for Edward. The earl of Northumberland and many other northern barons were killed. After the battle, other Lancastrians fled to Scotland with Margaret, Henry VI and their son, the young Prince Edward. Edward earl of March was confirmed as king, and crowned as Edward IV on 28 June 1461.

The first reign of Edward IV, 1461–69

Edward IV had both to consolidate the position which he had won at Towton and re-establish the authority of a crown weakened by years of disorder and by the disruption to orderly government caused by Queen Margaret's withdrawal from Westminster for prolonged periods, which had paralysed many of the normal routines. Although these themes will be discussed separately, they were not separate in fact and constantly interacted with each other.

The consolidation of the victory at Towton

Many leading Lancastrians had been killed at Towton; others, such as the dukes of Exeter and Somerset, had escaped to Scotland with Queen Margaret, Henry VI and Prince Edward, while Jasper Tudor, who had a considerable following in Wales, was also at liberty. Edward controlled the south-east, and for the moment

Yorkshire was cowed by the losses at Towton. Elsewhere, Edward still had to fight for control.

The Lancastrian exiles in Scotland concentrated their efforts mainly in the north, a region in which Edward himself seemed not to be very interested. Most of the fighting there was directed for the Yorkists by Warwick and his brother, John Neville, Lord Montague. By 1464, Montague's military flair had finally secured the Northumbrian castles, Warkworth, Alnwick and Dunstanburgh; but it was a hard struggle and they changed hands many times before Montague's final victory at Hexham on 15 May 1464. Montague then received, in reward, the Percy earldom of Northumberland. In the following year, 1465, Henry VI, who had returned to England during these Lancastrian invasions of the north and remained in hiding after their defeat, was captured in west Yorkshire by supporters of Edward IV and imprisoned in the Tower, where he remained till 1470. The establishment of Yorkist authority in Wales took longer. It was not until 1468 that William Herbert, one of Edward's most trusted agents, was able to oust Jasper Tudor from Harlech, the last Lancastrian stronghold. Herbert was rewarded with Jasper's earldom of Pembroke. Jasper himself escaped to France.

The establishment of Yorkist government

Edward IV personally gave more attention to establishing his overall authority. He aimed to assert himself where lawlessness and disorder had flourished, for example in East Anglia, where he intervened personally to restore order in 1461. There Lancastrian courtiers had been able to behave more or less as they liked until Edward reasserted royal authority. He also made great efforts to reconcile former Lancastrians. Some simply took advantage of this to rebel. But many of Edward's attempts at reconciliation were successful.

Edward also had to build up a circle of men loyal to himself, both at a national level, where he promoted and endowed men like William Hastings, who became his Chamberlain in 1461, William Herbert, Lord Audley, Sir Walter Devereux and Sir John Howard, and in the localities, where royal favour could help to secure many advantages. Thus, in the early 1460s, Edward was establishing a network of supporters who could make his rule effective. This was an essential step; but it was also important that they remained his servants and did not exploit his favour too blatantly, as some of Henry VI's courtiers had done.

Edward's marriage

Edward's marriage to Elizabeth Woodville in May 1464 might seem the most notable example of his policy of reconciliation. She was a widow with a large family from her previous marriage to Sir John Grey of Groby, a not particularly prominent Lancastrian who had been killed at the second battle of St Albans in 1461. She had been, it appears, a Lady of the Bedchamber to Henry VI's queen, Margaret of Anjou. However, to choose a widow with a large family from her previous marriage was completely outside the normal royal conventions. It was also done secretly (the marriage was not avowed until September) and entirely without the knowledge of any of the king's important servants or counsellors. Moreover, her large family rapidly made themselves unpopular by a series of marriages to prominent nobles and heiresses, to the displeasure of discomfited rivals. To any who were hostile to Edward IV, this might easily suggest a return to the bad old days of Henry VI's "court party".

The breakdown with Warwick

Edward's greatest difficulty was the increasing conflict with the earl of Warwick, who had played an important part in the Yorkist victory in 1461 and in the campaigns in the north in the early years of Edward's reign. The conflict culminated in Warwick's rebellion in 1469, and commentators then and since have tended to explain it as a result of Edward's marriage, which inevitably reduced Warwick's influence over the king. It is more likely however that the eventual breakdown occurred as a result of differences over foreign policy, in which Warwick had taken a special interest (see Chapter 5, pp. 63–6).

In the mid 1460s, England's foreign relations reached a turning point. Since the effective end of the Hundred Years' War in 1453, Lancastrian policy had tended towards developing good relations with France; and before Edward's eventual marriage, there had been negotiations for a French bride. However, Burgundy, once one of the great fiefs of France, had under Philip The Good (1419–67) become effectively a separate state, and in the 1460s, relations between the French crown and the duke of Burgundy deteriorated and were likely to deteriorate further under Philip's heir, Charles the Bold. This gave the Yorkists the option of either looking to France, or of supporting Burgundy in opposition. Their alliance was sought by both sides, and Edward was anxious to exploit the possibilities inherent in this situation.

Gradually, it emerged that Warwick, who headed numerous embassies in the period, favoured an alliance with France. Edward himself hesitated long, but, perhaps encouraged by the queen's family, gradually moved towards Burgundy, a move that was to be cemented by the marriage of his sister, Margaret, to Charles the Bold, by then duke, in 1468.

Warwick certainly took offence at this turn in foreign policy, and retired temporarily to his estates in the north. This was probably the essential cause of the rupture though it was not till 1469 that a decisive break occurred.

The years of crisis, 1469–71

The quarrel with Warwick, however, is not the whole explanation of the troubles that broke upon Edward IV in 1469. His government was increasingly unpopular. His reign, as it went on, seemed to many little better than Henry's; it was, according to one source, all battles, heavy taxation, and declining trade (Warkworth's Chronicle, in Dockray 1988: 34). In fact, Edward had been reasonably cautious over taxation. He waited till 1463 before imposing any taxes. He then obtained one-fifteenth and one-tenth, the standard tax on movables; in 1465 he received the grant of tonnage and poundage and the subsidy on wool (i.e. a grant of the customs) for life; and in 1468 two-fifteenths and two-tenths on the plea of a projected war with France. This was, however, a great deal more than Henry VI had ever obtained. There is also evidence of a resurgence of Lancastrian plots in 1468 and 1469. Without this basis of discontent, Warwick could have made no progress.

Serious trouble started with a confused series of northern revolts (there were probably three) in the early months of 1469. Some may have been inspired by Warwick; but at least one rising at York, led by an unknown calling himself "Robin of Holderness", may have originated in a purely local dispute over a customary levy to the hospital of St Leonard at York of 24 sheaves from each ploughland in a large surrounding area. Warwick, however, took advantage of the situation, and was able to win the support of Edward's brother, George, Duke of Clarence. There is no definite evidence as to why Clarence became disaffected at this time (but see below, p. 66).

In June of 1469 Warwick and Clarence openly joined forces and crossed to Warwick's stronghold of Calais, where Clarence and Warwick's eldest daughter Isabel were married, and on 12 July, a manifesto was issued in which Warwick and Clarence claimed to be acting against "certain seditious persons", whom they identified as almost all Edward's inner circle of counsellors, the leading Woodvilles, namely Earl Rivers and Anthony Woodville Lord Scales, as well as William Herbert, Earl of Pembroke, Lord Stafford, and others. They announced their intention to take up arms to rid the king of these evil advisers (Dockray 1988: 68–71).

Meanwhile, a group of the northern rebels under "Robin of Redesdale" (possibly Warwick's retainer Sir John Conyers), was advancing south in their second rising of the year. Edward called for support from Herbert in Wales, and from Lord Stafford. Warwick and Clarence now crossed to Kent, and, with very considerable support there, marched towards the king. All these forces converged on north Oxfordshire, though Edward himself remained inactive at Nottingham, awaiting the arrival of Herbert and Stafford. Redesdale's troops slipped past him to join Warwick and Clarence. The various armies met, in the absence of the king, at Edgecote near Banbury on 26 July, where Edward's supporters, Herbert and Stafford, were routed. Herbert was captured and executed the next day. Rivers and Sir John Woodville were later captured and executed on 12 August and Stafford was lynched at Bridgwater in Somerset on 17 August. Edward himself, unaware of what had happened, was captured by Warwick's brother, Archbishop George Neville, and taken to Warwick castle.

Warwick now controlled the king and had destroyed his leading advisers. His intention was apparently to take charge of the government in Edward's name. Warwick's triumph, however, soon evaporated, as it rapidly became clear that he did not possess the support of the groups that mattered, the greater nobles and the prominent gentry throughout the country. Lancastrian revolts broke out in the north, and, according to the Croyland Chronicler, Warwick found that he could not muster troops against them while Edward was a prisoner. A king who was Warwick's puppet would not be obeyed; consequently Warwick had to release Edward (Pronay & Cox 1986: 116–17).

For the next six months, Edward attempted once again to build bridges towards Warwick and Clarence, treating them as friends in public, though much less trustful than he had been. But trouble broke out again in the spring of 1470, with a rising in Lincolnshire, which may, like the 1469 rising in York, have originated in a local quarrel, in this case between a number of Lincolnshire landowners and a knight of the king's household, Sir Thomas à Burgh (Dockray 1988: 30). We do not know whether Warwick and Clarence stirred it up, or merely exploited it once it occurred. But Edward found, when he moved rapidly and forcefully against the rebels, that behind them stood Warwick and Clarence, with troops they had raised in the king's name. Edward, however, was too quick for them; before Warwick and Clarence could join the rebels, the men of Lincolnshire had been routed. Warwick's attempt collapsed, and he and Clarence had to flee abroad. There is no certain evidence of Warwick's aim in this rising. After his failure in 1469, he may have realised that he could not hope to rule in Edward's name; and may perhaps have hoped to depose Edward and place Clarence on the throne instead.

Warwick's first move was to try to return to his old base at Calais, but it remained loyal to Edward. Warwick therefore now had to withdraw to France; here, his old contact Louis XI brought about an almost incredible settlement, an agreement between Warwick and Margaret of Anjou to restore Henry VI to the throne! Once this agreement was achieved, Warwick, with Clarence, headed an invasion of England. Margaret remained in France till Henry should be restored. Warwick and Clarence landed in the West Country in mid-September 1470, and made their way directly to London. Edward was again in the north, whither he had gone to resist a Lancastrian rising which collapsed before he appeared. He remained confident that, in face of this new challenge, he could count on the support of Percy, whom he had just restored to the earldom of Northumberland, and of Warwick's brother, Montague, who had remained loyal to Edward through Warwick's earlier revolts. This time, however, Montague turned to support his brother, possibly because he had been forced to give up the earldom of Northumberland, which he had received as a reward for his efforts in the north in 1464. Although he had been compensated by being made a Marquess, he was clearly dissatisfied, and would no longer back Edward. Assuming that in this situation he was defenceless, Edward fled to King's Lynn with a few of his closest supporters, and managed to find a ship to take them to the Low Countries.

Warwick was able to bring Henry VI out of the Tower, where he was lodged, and restore him to the throne, in what is known as the "re-adeption" (an obsolete equivalent for "recovery") of Henry VI. Warwick's position, however, again proved weak. Margaret, her son Prince Edward and other Lancastrian exiles were still in France. Warwick was distrusted by the Lancastrians in England, and, it seems, no more accepted by the mass of the nobility than he had been the previous year. Henry VI was an acceptable figurehead, but everyone knew that he was not directing affairs.

Clarence was also marginalized by events. There was very little for him in the Lancastrian restoration, and very quickly Edward's agents were trying to lure him back. Edward himself was for a time in limbo, since his hopes depended on Charles the Bold of Burgundy, who was in no hurry to get involved; but Charles's attitude changed when, in December 1470, Louis XI decided on an open attack on Burgundy. Thereafter, Charles had every reason to support Edward in order to detach England from France; in March Edward was able to set sail with some Burgundian support.

An attempt to land in East Anglia found the area held by strong Lancastrians. A second attempt at Ravenspur was more successful, but to survive Edward had to pretend to have abandoned any claim to the throne, and to be seeking only his duchy of York. Even so, he was grudgingly received. But the earl of Northumberland held off his men from opposing Edward, and, for whatever reason, Montague did the same. In the Midlands, Edward had better fortune as supporters began to come in, and by the time Edward confronted

Warwick at Coventry, he was sufficiently strong that Warwick hesitated to emerge from his defensible position in the town.

At this point, Clarence rejoined Edward, who now had a substantial force and rightly decided to ignore Warwick, heading instead directly for London. The capital, as it happened, was not seriously defended. The Lancastrian leaders there had learned that Margaret and Prince Edward were at last about to land in the west, and they left London to join her, leaving only Warwick's brother, Archbishop Neville, to hold the capital. He made an attempt to rally support from the Londoners, but this failed. This disorganization of the Lancastrian effort was to be the salvation of Edward.

He seized London, where he was in any case welcome, and returned Henry to the Tower. Without hesitation, he headed north to confront Warwick, who had followed him from Coventry. They met at Barnet on 14 April where both Warwick and Montague were killed in a hard-fought battle in a dense fog. Edward then, with barely a pause, went west to catch up with Margaret, who had meantime landed at Weymouth. She was now collecting forces and heading north towards Wales, where she expected further support, thanks to Jasper Tudor's influence. A brilliant series of forced marches, and some very shrewd or lucky guesses at her plans, enabled Edward to catch up with the Lancastrian forces outside Tewkesbury, where he won his final decisive victory on 4 May. Prince Edward and several other Lancastrian leaders were killed in the battle; the duke of Somerset and other notable prisoners were executed two days later and Margaret herself was captured.

Tewkesbury finally destroyed the Lancastrian cause, but there was still a group of Kentish rebels, devotees of Warwick, under Thomas Neville, the bastard son of William Neville Lord Fauconberg, who were attacking London. Edward therefore hastened back to the capital, to find the rebellion had melted away as he drew near. A brief stop coincided with the death of Henry VI in the Tower "of pure displeasure and melancholy", according to an official Yorkist source (Dockray 1988: 184). Edward went on to suppress the remaining Kentish rebels.

By the end of May 1471, Edward was unchallenged. The only prominent and active Lancastrians left, Jasper Tudor, Henry Earl of Richmond (the future Henry VII) and the Earl of Oxford, were in hiding or had already fled abroad, where their capacity to threaten the Yorkist throne was at an end, at least until after Edward's death in 1483.

The second reign of Edward IV, 1471–83

For the remaining 12 years of Edward's reign, the Yorkist dynasty seemed secure. Edward did all he could to win over those who had supported Henry VI and most accepted. They had nothing else to hope for. Much of his effort in those years was devoted to foreign policy and to the development of Yorkist government, including the establishment of order and royal authority in Wales and the north, both areas which had been centres of trouble in his previous reign (see below p. 68). The arrangements he made for these regions were to provide precedents for the Tudors. In the general history of England, these are the important themes but they are not directly relevant to the Wars of the Roses.

Two developments, however, were to be of great significance for events after Edward's death: the rise of his younger brother, Richard Duke of Gloucester, to become the most prominent agent of Edward's rule; and Edward's final clash with his brother, George Duke of Clarence.

Richard had already, even in his teens, won Edward's confidence as a trusted supporter in the years of troubles. After Warwick's death, Richard replaced him for a short time as the king's leading agent in Wales; subsequently, he was given Warwick's lands in the north and began the process over ten years of building up his position there, for the most part in co-operation with the earl of Northumberland, with whom he shared the wardenships of the marches. Eventually, he also had to handle the increasingly difficult relations with Scotland, culminating in a not very successful invasion of that country in 1482. He was at least able to restore English control of Berwick, which had been in Scottish hands since 1461.

In this period, Richard built up for himself a following in the north, mainly from former retainers of Warwick who came over to him with the lands, and whose loyalty he seems to have been able to win and hold (Horrox 1989). At the same time, he continued to play an important part in the general government of England.

The other issue which was to have repercussions after 1483 was the collapse of relations with Clarence. This began in heated quarrels with Richard over the inheritance from Warwick. Clarence, as the husband of Warwick's elder daughter, clearly wished to take over Warwick's position. Richard, however, despite strong hostility from Clarence, married the second daughter, Anne, the widow of Henry VI's son, Prince Edward. The quarrel was so violent that it took Edward several years to settle it, and Richard had to make considerable concessions.

These evidently did not satisfy Clarence, who continued to act in an overbearing manner, and was indeed suspected of dealings with the exiled Lancastrian earl of Oxford, and of spreading rumours discreditable to Edward. In 1476, Clarence's wife Isabel died. Clarence himself now covertly sought a marriage with the daughter and heiress of Charles the Bold of Burgundy, a scheme which Edward rejected. He distrusted Clarence too much to allow him such a powerful prospect. Clarence then proceeded, quite illegally, to seize his late wife's nurse, Ankarette Twynho, from her home in Somerset. carry her off to Warwick, and force a jury to convict her of Isabel's murder, for which she was immediately executed. The records provide no evidence to support this charge, and no convincing explanation of Clarence's behaviour has ever been advanced. It seems that this was too much for Edward. Soon after Ankarette's execution, a pair of "astronomers" (necromancers?) and a servant of Clarence's, Thomas Burdett, were accused of plotting Edward's death by necromancy, and two of them, Burdett and a Dr John Stacey, were executed. It has been suggested that this was intended as a warning to Clarence (Ross 1974: 240–1). If so, Clarence ignored the warning and made a formal protest to the Council.

The consequence was that, in the summer of 1477, Edward had Clarence arrested, and charged with multiple treasons. He was condemned to death in a parliament in 1478; and secretly executed some weeks later.

The account given by Dominic Mancini, writing in 1483, of the background to events after Edward IV's death suggests that Clarence's death created a breech between Richard of Gloucester and the queen, Elizabeth Woodville, and her family. According to Mancini, Richard blamed the Woodvilles for Clarence's death and withdrew from court in disgust for the rest of the reign. This, however, may well be a version put about by Richard's supporters in 1483 to justify his actions against members of the Woodville family. There is no explicit evidence that they were responsible for Clarence's death: the Croyland Chronicle attributes that to Edward himself (Pronay and Cox 1986: 144–7). Nor does it seem true, as Mancini says, that Richard was alienated from court after his brother's death. He indeed spent most of his time in the rest of his brother's reign in the north of England, but that was as Edward's continuing agent in these parts. Richard's position there was not a withdrawal but an essential part of Edward's plans for the maintenance of royal authority (see below p. 68; and Horrox 1989, Chapter 1).

Other lesser quarrels were almost inevitable in a fifteenth-century court. Most significant for the future were those between some of Edward's closest advisers, notably William Hastings, his chamberlain, and members of the Woodville family. Tensions were clearly developing at the Yorkist court. They would probably not have mattered if Edward had not fallen unexpectedly ill in the early months of 1483 and died on 9 April.

The usurpation and reign of Richard III, 1483–85

At this point, many of those who expected to be in control of affairs during the minority of Edward's son, the young Edward V, were scattered over the country. The new king himself, under the care of Earl Rivers, the queen's brother, was at Ludlow in the Welsh March. His uncle, Richard Duke of Gloucester, was on his Yorkshire estates; while the duke of Buckingham, after Richard the most prominent noble of full age in the kingdom, was probably on his estates on the Welsh March.

We do not know precisely what arrangements Edward had made for the custody of his son. The Woodville family was anxious to retain control of the young king, but other counsellors, headed by William Hastings, seem to have wished to limit Woodville influence. Those who were not in London depended on letters for their news of what was happening.

All actors moved towards the capital. Richard and Buckingham met at Northampton, presumably by arrangement. There, they were joined on 29 May by Earl Rivers, who had travelled to greet them from Stony Stratford where the young king and his company had rested. This meeting too was probably pre-arranged.

The following morning, however, Richard and Buckingham arrested Rivers and two of his companions, and sent them off to prison in Yorkshire. No clear reason was given. This may have been Richard's first move to clear his way to the throne; or a defensive move in face of what he took to be a Woodville threat to himself. Richard and Buckingham then went on towards London with the young king.

The news of these arrests threw London into disarray. The queen and her family took sanctuary in Westminster Abbey. Members of the council debated how to react, but were apparently calmed by assurances from Hastings that Richard had no further violent plans. When he arrived in London, preparations went forward for the new king's coronation, though the queen and the king's brother remained in sanctuary.

Richard took no further dramatic action till about 10 June; this may mean that it was only then that he discovered his "right" to the throne, based on the story of the alleged illegitimacy of the princes. It may mean, as he claimed, that he then suddenly discovered evidence of a plot against himself by Hastings and the queen, or it may simply mean that his covert preparations for the coup which followed were only then complete.

On 10 June, Richard hastily summoned assistance from the city of York, and from his other well-wishers in the north, assistance which could not arrive until the coup was well advanced. On 13 June, at a council meeting, he arrested and summarily executed Hastings. On 16 June, a party of troops descended on Westminster and forced the queen to surrender the Duke of York, who was lodged in the Tower with his brother the young king. A preacher was persuaded to publish Richard's claim to the throne at St Paul's Cross; Buckingham took charge of informal meetings in London which were with difficulty persuaded to accept Richard's claim. On 26 June, Richard was formally enthroned. He was crowned as Richard III on 6 July. Dominic Mancini commented that after Hasting's death, all were too cowed to resist (Armstrong 1969: 96–7). The young king and his brother remained in the Tower, to meet a fate which remains in detail uncertain.

This coup had proved impossible to resist. It had, however, consequences for Richard's rule. There were those among Edward's close advisers who gave their loyalty to Richard, notably John Lord Howard, who, on 28 June, became the first Howard Duke of Norfolk, a title to which he had a claim. But most of Edward's courtiers were dismayed at the rumours of the death of Edward's sons. Many of them launched a revolt against Richard in the autumn, at first on behalf of Edward V. Subsequently this was joined by the Duke of Buckingham, who had more than anyone put Richard on the throne. When it was understood that the princes were dead, the rebels turned to the only direct claimant to the throne not in Richard's hands, Henry Earl of Richmond, an exile in Brittany since 1471. He set out to join them in November; but Richard and Norfolk had very effectively crushed the revolt by then, and most of the rebels simply fled overseas to join Richmond. He had been warned in time, and returned to Normandy, and thence to Brittany. Buckingham was captured and executed.

Richard had demonstrated his grip; but his rule was faced with great difficulties. Many of the influential gentry of the south, who had family connections with the Woodvilles and were loyal to the memory of Edward IV, were now in exile. Richard had to depend far more on his northern retainers, who proved unpopular in the south. Nevertheless, his authority was effective. He was able to convene a parliament in 1484, in which some minor but useful reforms in the law of uses and conveyancing were developed along with the inevitable attainders and forfeitures of the rebels. Even those, like the Stanleys, and perhaps the earl of Northumberland, who were hesitant, were perforce loyal. For long the prospects of Richmond seemed very slim. By the end of 1484, even Edward IV's widow, Queen Elizabeth Woodville, was prepared to compromise, and her daughters joined Richard's court for the Christmas festivities. This was a particular blow to Richmond, who planned to marry the eldest daughter, also called Elizabeth, to bolster his claim, and to win over the loyalty of the former Yorkists.

In 1484, however, Richard's only son died; a year later his wife also died. At this point, Richard had the idea that he might marry his niece, Edward IV's daughter Elizabeth, and so baulk any plans Richmond had in that direction. But Richard's own followers would not tolerate this. This left Richard without an immediate heir. Even so, Richmond had little force, and no military experience of consequence, while Richard was battle tried and had shown grasp and energy in the suppression of the rebellion on 1483.

Henry's invasion, when it came in the early autumn of 1485, did not start off well. Although Richard had to defend a whole coast-line, and so was not ready at the right place, supporters for Richmond came in very slowly when he first landed in west Wales. Worse, the Stanleys on whose backing he counted, were cautious; Richard held Lord Stanley's son as hostage, and they would not declare for Richmond.

The result of Bosworth was not foregone. Everything was to fight for, and the report is that both Richard and Norfolk fought manfully. Yet on the day Henry triumphed, and the Stanleys' eventual move in his favour settled the matter. Richard and Norfolk were both killed, and Richmond was left, according to legend, to be crowned with Richard's battle-crown by Stanley on the field.

Epilogue, 1485–99

With Bosworth, we tend to regard the Wars of the Roses as over. With the death of Richard III without a direct heir, the chief male line of the house of York came to an end. Henry, as he had promised, married Edward IV's daughter Elizabeth, to conciliate the many Yorkists who had deserted Richard. Yet it was to be some time before Henry VII could feel secure. There was to be little support for a Yorkist restoration in England, but in Ireland, the backing which Duke Richard of York had given to the native nobility when he was Lieutenant in the 1450s had won a lasting sympathy for his family. Henry VII's foreign enemies, in France, Burgundy and Scotland, could still stir up trouble.

Henry VII faced three Yorkist rebellions. The first, in 1486, by Lord Lovell and the Staffords, followers of Richard III, quickly collapsed. The second was more serious. It began in Ireland, around the impostor Lambert Simnel, who pretended to be Clarence's son, the earl of Warwick (the real Warwick was imprisoned in the Tower). On his behalf there emerged a rising of Irish lords, supported by Yorkist sympathizers in England headed by the earl of Lincoln, the son of Edward IV's sister Elizabeth, and heir-presumptive to Richard III since the death of his own son in 1484. This was a serious challenge which culminated in the hard-fought battle of Stoke in June 1487. The result was a decisive victory for Henry and the end of the rising. Lincoln and several other leaders were killed.

Thereafter, the risings headed by another impostor, Perkin Warbeck, who claimed to be the younger of the "Princes in the Tower", proved much less serious, since they found little support in England. Warbeck was supported by Edward IV's sister, Margaret of Burgundy, and, when it suited them, by the kings of Scots and France. An invasion from Scotland in 1495, with some support from its king, James IV, collapsed within a few miles. In 1497, Warbeck tried to revive a quite unconnected Cornish rebellion, which had just been suppressed, but again got little support, and was forced to surrender. He was then lodged in the Tower, whence he, and apparently the young earl of Warwick, Clarence's son, who was also in the Tower, tried to stir up further plots. In 1499, both were executed.

After Stoke in 1487, the Wars of the Roses were effectively at an end, though embers could still occasionally flicker, and Henry VIII remained for decades nervous of the danger. Nothing, however, quite like the disturbances of the period 1450 to 1487 was to recur.

CHAPTER 3

The social and political situation in the fifteenth century

The events of the years 1450 to 1485 and beyond were certainly dramatic. At no other period since the Norman Conquest had turmoil been so prolonged or drastic; it is tempting therefore to look for causes peculiar to the age. Was there something that made the mid-fifteenth century especially liable to political upheavals? As we have seen already, to Tudor writers the causes were simple. The Wars of the Roses were a consequence of the usurpation of 1399, and were brought to an end when the first Tudor, Henry VII, joined together the two rival houses and so removed the essential cause of strife. It is hard now to accept so straightforward an explanation. Henry IV's usurpation may have depended on a flawed title, but he was accepted at the time. Like the later usurpers, Edward IV and Richard III, he had to destroy opposition by force; but he did so, and he died secure on the throne. It was not till his son and grandson had reigned for almost 40 years that any challenge emerged to the Lancastrian title. The Yorkists had indeed a better claim than the Lancastrians, because they were descended from Lionel, Duke of Clarence, the second surviving son of Edward III, while the Lancastrians were descended from John of Gaunt, the third son (see Genealogical Table, pp. x–xi); but that had no practical effect till after 1450.

Other general explanations for the political upheavals of the period have often been suggested: first, the consequences of the collapse of the English conquests in the 1440s and 50s at the end of the Hundred Years' War; secondly, the upheavals in medieval society which originated in the famines and plagues of the fourteenth century, and may have had the effect of destabilizing what may have been the more settled society of the thirteenth century; and thirdly, the economic situation in the mid-fifteenth century itself. None of these can by themselves explain adequately what happened in the 1450s and following decades, but all might have contributed towards a more volatile and dangerous political situation.

The failures in France certainly did so. To us, the Hundred Years' War must seem a futile enterprise heading for inevitable disaster, but it did not necessarily seem so to contemporaries. Our instinct is to applaud Henry VI's desire for peace, even if we recognize that he proved incompetent in seeking it. But his subjects remembered the triumphs of his father, Henry V, who died, by a stroke of ill fate, only just before he was due to inherit the throne of France. We can now see how much his apparent triumph depended on civil war in France and on the support of Duke Philip the Good of Burgundy. We can also recognize how much Henry V still had to do, were he to become effective ruler of the whole of France. Yet none of this prevented the first 30 years of Henry VI's reign from seeming a sad anticlimax. By the 1450s, national pride had suffered a succession of blows: the surrender of Maine in 1448, the loss of Normandy in 1450 and the final loss of Bordeaux in 1453. Every version of the complaints put forward by the rebels in 1450 harps on the losses in France; to quote a typical passage:

> Also the Realm of France, the Duchy of Normandy, Gascony, and Guyennne, Anjou and Maine lost by the same traitors [those who have misadvised Henry VI], and our true lords and knights, squires and good yeomen lost and sold ere they went over the sea, which is great pity and great loss to our sovereign lord and destruction to his realm (Harvey 1991: 191).

Henry V's triumphs proved delusive, in that they left an illusion of the possibility of victory which was to dog his son's reign.

More was at stake than national pride. As K. B. McFarlane strenuously argued, it was the hope of profit that mainly attracted the nobility and gentry to the French war, profits from ransoms, to a lesser degree booty, and also from offices and lands acquired in the captured regions. (See the essays "War, the economy and social change", "A business partnership in war and administration,

1421–1445" and "The investment of Sir John Fastolf's profits of war" in K. B. McFarlane 1981: 139–97). Evidence for the extent of these gains is scanty, but in the next century their profits were believed to have been great. However, we know something of one case. There is evidence of the sums Sir John Fastolf was able to transfer to England from his winnings abroad. We know that he rose from relatively humble origins to build Caister Castle in Norfolk, and to become a notable East Anglian landowner. McFarlane was able to identify at least some of the profits which Fastolf was able to remit, even as late as the 1440s. Yet, though his rewards were great, and though he was successful in selling some at least of his French lands before the collapse, in McFarlane's words, "the surrender of Maine and the fall of Normandy deprived him of what was left. The events of 1449–50 involved Fastolf and others like him in heavy and sudden financial loss. No wonder that the dispossessed wanted Suffolk's blood!" (McFarlane 1981: 188).

Fastolf's gains were probably greater than those of many; but C. T. Allmand has shown how important was the hope of acquiring French lands for those who took part in the war. Many of these lands, abandoned by their French owners as a result of the English conquests, were granted by Henry V as a direct reward for service; but others had been bought from the original grantees as an investment (Allmand 1968: 462–9). By the 1440s, returns were tiny or nil. Naturally such lands were in the end hard to sell. One William Bronfield was reduced in 1445 to trying to sell part of his French lands on the terms that he would take them back and refund the purchase price if the buyer found them unprofitable! (ibid: 475). As Allmand observes, "Such men felt cheated and betrayed" (ibid: 479) by the collapse of the English effort in France.

The failures in the French war provided the immediate occasion for the furious impeachment in 1450 of Henry VI's leading minister, William de la Pole, Duke of Suffolk and his lynching on the way to exile after it. They also contributed substantially to the discontent expressed in Jack Cade's rebellion in May and June of the same year. So complete and, in the end, sudden were the disasters of the late 1440s that it was hardly surprising that they should seem the work of traitors. The final collapse of the attempt to conquer France which had dominated English policy for so long, aroused shame and fury against those who might be held responsible. It certainly played a part in destabilizing the political world of the 1450s.

The mid-fifteenth century was also a difficult time in the economic life of England. It was a period of great economic changes, which affected both the patterns of rural life and the economies of the towns. Such changes inevitably contributed to the stresses and tensions which underlay the political problems of the time.

The rural economy had been profoundly changed by the famines of the early fourteenth century and by the even greater cataclysm of the recurrent plagues which began with the Black Death in 1348/49 and continued intermittently through the rest of the century. An economy which had been built on a steadily expanding population for some three centuries before 1300 had been thrown into reverse by the decline in population which accompanied these natural disasters. In the long run, the change seems to have improved the condition of the peasantry. With fewer people to depend on the land, the livelihood of each improved; and for some there was the opportunity to extend their lands by acquiring vacant tenements, and so make possible a rise in social status into the ranks of the gentry, the lesser landholding class. Some of the gentry families of the fifteenth century were sprung from the peasantry. Enemies of the Pastons claimed that they were descended from a bondman who lived in the late fourteenth century. This may or may not be true; the account was clearly written to denigrate the family in the course of a bitter legal dispute (Gairdner 1904, i: 28–30), but it was at least socially plausible. The Catesbies of Coventry were another family who rose from humble origins slightly earlier than the Pastons. The Black Death certainly made profound changes in the social structures of England.

It is also possible that the plague may have affected the economic dominance of the greater landowners. An immediate consequence of the Black Death was a dearth of tenant labourers to work the great estates, ecclesiastical and lay. The Statute of Labourers of 1351 was an attempt to reassert the landlords' control over their tenants by regulating wages and prices, and preventing labourers from leaving the service of their lords, or, in the case of journeymen, their masters. There is evidence that tenants still tried to escape from their burdens. In the mid-1370s groups of them in the south of England took out "exemplifications" (certified extracts) of passages in Domesday in what may have been an attempt to argue at law that they were not subject to some or other burdens. There were complaints about their efforts in the parliament of 1377. The Great Revolt of 1381 was also in some measure an attempt to bring an end to villeinage; its abolition was one of the main demands which the young Richard II had to grant in his attempt to pacify the rebels. The attempt failed in the short term, since the concessions were revoked once the emergency had passed, but villeinage does seem to have disappeared relatively quickly thereafter, as lords increasingly found it was easier to become rentiers and give up the direct exploitation of their demesnes. These passed into the hands of "farmers", tenants paying fixed rents. This did not necessarily damage the economic position of the lords; there is little evidence of poverty among the fifteenth-century aristocracy (McFarlane 1981: 240). One's first impression is rather of their capacity for lavish spending to bolster their status. But the sense of direct lordship over a dependent tenantry was much weakened.

There were also particularly severe economic problems in the mid-fifteenth century. At that time, the towns were being affected by changes in the patterns of overseas trade. The east coast ports had built their prosperity on the wool trade, exporting English wool to the great cloth-making towns of Flanders. In the fourteenth century, these manufacturing centres began to decline, partly because of social troubles, and partly because of the Hundred Years' War. This gave English weavers the opportunity to break into an international trade in cloth from which they had previously been excluded. Gradually the wool trade declined and cloth manufacture prospered, till by the fifteenth century the cloth trade was dominant. But the profits of that went to the areas where cloth was manufactured, the Cotswolds, rural East Anglia, and, as the fifteenth century progressed, the more upland towns which were developing in Yorkshire, all areas where wool and water power for the fulling mills could be brought together. This was a shift in prosperity rather than a decline, but for the east coast ports like King's Lynn and Boston, and, in the fifteenth century, for York, the loss was serious. It was small comfort to these towns to know that their decline was balanced by the dramatic gains of places such as Chipping Camden, Castle Combe, Lavenham, Wakefield, Leeds and Bradford.

How far can we relate these changes to the political tensions which provoked the outbreaks of the 1450s? That decade was a period of particular depression, in some respects deepened by the loss of the English provinces in France. Normandy (finally lost in 1450) and the Pas de Calais (by then reduced to the Pale of Calais itself) had provided access to the markets of northern France and the Burgundian Netherlands, while the wine trade depended heavily on access to the wine producing areas of Gascony (finally lost in 1453). All these losses reduced the scope for English trade and profits. Yet it is not easy to make a direct connection with the civil wars. Some nobles, such as the Earl of Warwick, and even King Edward IV, did engage in trade, but luxury trade was mainly an activity of wealthy merchants, particularly London merchants. The towns in general took little if any part in provoking civil war and disturbance. They were concerned with trade, local and national, and wanted peace and the opportunity for profit. Wars, whether in France or England, did not suit them. Admittedly Londoners had a definite tendency to support the Yorkists, particularly financially, but this was at least partly because of the tendency of the Lancastrians in the 1450s to remove the court and the centre of government to the Midlands. This move hit the Londoners hard, since they had profited greatly from the presence of the court and government. But the habit of merchants was always and naturally to lie low in times of trouble, and to accept and work with the group in power. They did not want the wars, and did nothing to provoke them.

Beyond these economic problems, however, were there more fundamental elements of instability in the society of the mid-fifteenth century?

When we look in any detail at the behaviour and attitudes of the gentry, the men at the base of the political system in the fifteenth century, stability and order is not our first impression. Our fullest and most vivid source, the *Paston Letters*, certainly has its share of political agitations, protests, violence, the odd murder, and even a full scale siege of one of their manors (see Gairdner 1904 and Davis 1971–76). They may not be typical: the Pastons were on the make (in the late seventeenth century they reached the ranks of the nobility, though the family became extinct soon afterwards) and some of their attempts to advance themselves look distinctly dubious.

Their claim to control the inheritance of Sir John Fastolf in their own interest aroused hostility at the time, and to this day looks close to dishonesty. It is perhaps not surprising that they attracted hostility and enmity. Nonetheless, meticulous and thorough studies of the gentry of Derbyshire and Warwickshire (Wright 1983, Carpenter 1992) provide examples in plenty of the kind of litigation, quarrels tending to violence, and of what is at times a frantic search for patronage and support from the influential, with which readers of the *Paston Letters* are familiar. The Pastons may be an extreme case, but the Catesbies and the Mountfords in Warwickshire, the Blounts and the Vernons in Derbyshire, were living in the same world, and it was neither stable nor orderly.

Nor were the quarrels and conflicts of the gentry little local difficulties which did not affect the world of high politics. They were men who mattered in politics; in aggregate, they held much more land than the lords, and they were not necessarily easily led. Their primary interests were in their families and their lands, in advancing their position and wealth. To that end, they often sought "lordship", the support and backing of the great.

There is a good example of the attempted use of influence in a letter of John Paston, the younger son of the first John Paston to figure in the letters. It was addressed to his mother Margaret in 1479. His brother, Sir John, had just died and there was a family quarrel over some of his estates. In this crisis, John wrote:

> But this I think to do when I come to London to speak with my Lord Chamberlain [this was William Hastings, close confidant of the king and long a contact of John Paston, though not, so far as we know, his lord], and to win by his means my Lord of Ely [John Morton, bishop of Ely], if I can; and if I may by any of their means cause the king to take my service and my quarrell together, I will, and I think that Sir George Brown, Sir James Radclyff, and other of mine aquaintance, which wait most upon the king, and lie nightly in his chamber [i.e. were Knights of the Chamber], will put to their good wills. This is my way as yet. (Gairdner 1904, no.962, vol. vi: 28–9)

John Paston was using all the influence he had and seeking all the lordship he could get in order to advance his chances in a family dispute. This is how influence and lordship worked.

Lordship was important to the gentry, but it was anything but stable, as they would not necessarily do what their lords wanted. There is a very pertinent comment in the official account of Edward IV's recovery of the crown in 1471, *The Arrival of King Edward IV* (Dockray 1988: 152–3). When Edward IV landed at Ravenspur in Yorkshire, he was, as we have seen, so weak that he had to disclaim any designs on the throne, and profess only to seek his restoration as Duke of York. The Percy Earl of Northumberland was the most powerful noble in the area, and was allegedly well disposed towards Edward. Yet even he could not bring his followers on to Edward's side. This was, according to *The Arrival*, because they remembered the battle of Towton (in 1461) in which "their master, the earl's father, was slain, many of their fathers, their sons, their brethren and kinsmen, and other many of their neighbours." Therefore they would not give their support to Edward now, and Northumberland could not make them.

Their unwillingness to be involved was more typical than is often believed. Christine Carpenter has pointed out that very few of the Warwickshire gentry were prepared to support either side in the crucial conflicts of 1460 and 1461 in the battles of Northampton, Wakefield, the second battle of St Albans, and Towton, even though the dominant nobleman in Warwickshire was Warwick the Kingmaker, irretrievably committed at that point to the Yorkist side (Carpenter 1992: 481–6). In 1485, it was Richard III who controlled the earldom of Warwick, then in the hands of the Crown; but there were few Warwickshire gentry fighting for him at Bosworth (ibid: 559). In Norfolk, John Paston seems to have been regarded as a probable supporter by John Howard, created Duke of Norfolk by Richard III. Norfolk twice wrote calling on Paston to turn out with as many men as he could, once against the rebels of 1483, and lastly for Bosworth (Gairdner, 1904, 994, 1002, vi: 73, 85). We do not know his response in 1483, but it is unlikely that he turned out in 1485, since he emerges almost at once as sheriff of Norfolk under Henry VII.

These are cases where we may assume inactivity. There are others where gentry reacted against their supposed affinity. The most obvious is in 1483, when Richard III, who had been such an important figure in Edward IV's royal affinity, became king and so inherited control of the whole of that affinity. These bonds did not prevent very large numbers of the royal affinity, both at court and in the counties, supporting "Buckingham's" rebellion in October (Horrox 1989, Chapter 3).

Retinues in the fifteenth century were clearly not stable entities on which lords could rely. As Christine Carpenter has very clearly shown, and as we can see from all these examples, the gentry had interests and minds of their own. They would be loyal to lords where they found it advantageous, but maintaining oneself as head of an affinity involved hard work, and considerable political understanding. Of all the earls of Warwick covered in Dr Carpenter's study, only Richard Beauchamp, Earl of Warwick from 1403 to 1439, and in the periods when the earldom was in royal hands, Edward IV, were clearly able to maintain order and control the county. Warwick the Kingmaker, Clarence, Richard III, and even, in her view, Henry VII, conspicuously failed to retain the loyalty of the Warwickshire gentry.

Fifteenth-century gentry were likely to pursue their own paths in any crisis. Did this independence in fact threaten the position and influence of the nobility, weaken their dominance, and so make them more inclined than at other periods to resort to violent and aggressive behaviour? Should we see the Wars of the Roses as a desperate effort on the part of the nobility to restore a position and status which they felt to be crumbling?

There is a certain plausibility in this suggestion, but only in rather particular circumstances. The nobility were normally the channel through which royal authority percolated into the localities. It was on them that the king had to depend to raise armies when he needed them; and to back up and enforce the authority of his servants in the shires. Their power to do both these things depended on their influence over the gentry in the regions where they were great landowners and especially over the members of their affinities, whose loyalty they had to retain. To do that, the nobility had to be able to render services of value to the members of those affinities, particularly to support them in the many quarrels and disputes prevalent in a landed society. Justice in the Middle Ages depended on influence. The favour of the sheriff was essential in a lawsuit, for he was responsible for empanelling juries and had to serve and execute the writs which were essential to the process. A powerful lord could guarantee the support of sheriffs within his area; a lord of good standing at court could also use his influence at times in the interests of members of his affinity. Normally, this, in our eyes, corrupt system worked smoothly enough. It was well understood that "good lordship" was essential to maintain the position of families such as the Pastons and others who have been studied in Warwickshire, Derbyshire and elsewhere.

These rather complex systems of influence could crumble. A lord who was himself bad at handling his affinity, who proved ineffective in resolving disputes among his retainers or supporting them when they needed him, might find his authority collapsing. A lord who was denied influence at court, perhaps because the king's attention and influence was monopolized by too narrow a group of courtiers, might find that he could not render the support his retinue expected, especially if their troubles were essentially the result of the misdeeds of these same courtiers. Since these courtiers enjoyed the support of the crown, no other lord could provide any redress. In such circumstances no lord could feel secure in the loyalty of his affinity, and might easily be driven to violence at a national level in the attempt to recover it. It is certainly possible that these factors might directly have influenced the behaviour of both the Duke of York and the Earl of Warwick in their opposition to the court interest in the early 1450s.

Medieval society depended for its stability on the smooth working of these systems of influence, but this was not a problem peculiar to the mid-fifteenth century. We know much more about the volatility and independence of the gentry at that period than in earlier times because we know so much more about them. There are no earlier collections to match the Paston, Stonor and Plumpton letters. It is chiefly our lack of detailed information that makes earlier medieval politics seem so much more exclusively an affair of kings and nobles. The studies of Nigel Saul and Michael Bennett (Saul 1981, Bennett 1983) take the independent gentry well back into the fourteenth century; work on the thirteenth century has long emphasized the importance of the "knights" in the politics of the barons' wars; and J. R. Maddicott's essay on "Magna Carta and the local community 1215–1259" (Maddicott 1984) makes the point that King John had to deal with independent-minded county communities. If we read Domesday aright, we discover that, although the survey is arranged under greater fiefs, even the

England of the Conqueror was a land held directly by a large body of comparatively modest landholders. The pattern of landholding revealed in Domesday is not all that different from that of the later Middle Ages. Kings and nobles at every period must have confronted the problem of maintaining the loyalty of these lesser gentry, whatever we choose to call them at particular periods. Some kings and some nobles were at all periods better at doing this than others.

As we shall see in Chapter 5, some kings, and indeed some nobles, were particularly bad at maintaining loyalty in the fifteenth century. But it is worth emphasizing that, even in the fifteenth century, some could maintain a stable society. Henry V was not only a charismatic leader in war; he could maintain his authority at home forcefully and effectively, as he showed in dealing with Sir John Oldcastle's rebellion at the beginning of 1414 and the Cambridge Plot in 1415 (Harriss 1985, Chapters 1, 2). Edward IV's second reign from 1471 to 1483 was a period of stability, disrupted only by the quarrels within the royal family itself (see Chapter 5 pp. 67–8). The Croyland Chronicle emphasizes the danger posed by the disagreements between Clarence and Gloucester; but Edward IV was able to weather those and also the greater threat of Clarence's own disloyalty. There is no sign there that fifteenth-century society was inherently ungovernable, and at the noble level, Richard Beauchamp (as Earl of Warwick during the reign of Henry V and the minority of Henry VI) and Lord Hastings in Derbyshire (in the second reign of Edward IV) were well able to control the gentry within their areas. Damping down and resolving disputes among the Warwickshire gentry caused the earl a good deal of trouble, but he was able to do it (Carpenter 1992: 365–93). Similarly Lord Hastings, who had not only his own lands but was also Steward of the Duchy of Lancaster lands in Derbyshire and the head of a notable affinity (Dunham 1955), was influential enough to hold the loyalty of his followers even when he was in exile with Edward IV in the winter of 1470–71, and to call them out in Edward's support in the campaign that culminated in the battles of Barnet and Tewkesbury in the spring of 1471. Some fifteenth-century nobles could maintain their authority without violence. It required an understanding of the system and the ability to work it.

The more we learn of the local politics of the fifteenth century, the more it seems that disaster, when it came, was the result of the incapacity of those who should have had the authority to maintain stability. But there were other aspects of the medieval polity which at least exposed it to the danger of collapse. These aspects were by no means peculiar to the fifteenth century. They had caused crises many times already and were to continue to do so for some centuries more. To these more general aspects we must now turn before we can see what actually went wrong in the period of the Wars of the Roses.

CHAPTER 4

The problem of authority in the middle ages

The period from 1450 to 1485 saw successive collapses of royal authority, from the revolt of Jack Cade in 1450 to Buckingham's rebellion in 1483 and the invasion by Richmond in 1485, culminating in Richard III's defeat and death at Bosworth. Such a series of revolutions was hard to parallel, but the fundamental problem, that opposition and discontent was often expressed in baronial revolt, was by no means confined to the mid-fifteenth century. It was a recurrent feature of medieval political life. Even William the Conqueror faced one rebellion in 1075; Henry I more than one in the years after 1102; Stephen's reign was almost all revolts; Henry II faced one in 1173–74, as did those in charge of England during the absence of Richard I from 1192–94; King John notoriously in 1215; Henry III a long series from 1258 to 1265; Edward II three, in 1311, 1321–22, and finally in 1326–27; Richard II two, in 1387–88 and finally in 1399; Henry IV two, in 1403 and 1408. Only Edward I, Edward III and Henry V seemed generally exempt though even Edward I and Edward III faced baronial opposition, if not quite revolt, and Henry V was challenged, if only momentarily, by the Cambridge plot in 1415. If we are to understand the Wars of the Roses, we must recognize that they developed in a political system in which violent revolt was, and had long been, relatively common. We need to understand why this was so.

Medieval kings had no automatic power of coercion. The machinery of the modern estate to enforce its will – a professional police force and a standing army – did not exist. Royal authority, though in fact very powerful, was moral. Obedience was recognized as a duty and kings were recognized as almost religious figures. But they had no force at hand. Force depended on the readiness of their vassals, the nobles, to produce it, and their capacity to do so in turn depended on the willingness of lesser men to turn out when their support was called for. As we have seen, such backing was not automatic, but depended on good management and effective patronage. Therefore royal authority depended very much on the nobility. Kings like William the Conqueror, Henry I, Henry II, Edward I, Edward III and Henry V were generally secure in the support of the majority of their nobles. They were personally respected, and if some nobles tried to resist, these kings could generally call on enough support to quell any rising. Even Edward I, however, found in 1297 that he could go too far and had to climb down in face of very general protest. However masterful he usually was, he had the good sense to give way when necessary.

Conversely, the nobility lacked any political means to extract a remedy for their grievances. The king's will carried the force of law, and there was no formal provision for that will to be controlled. Kings did meet with their nobles in councils and parliaments, but kings usually regarded this as an occasion to express their will and they expected almost automatic consent. Such was the moral force behind their position that they usually obtained it. The development of parliament might seem to suggest a move to limit royal authority. Since the thirteenth century, one of the functions of parliaments in England had been the expression of grievances. By the fourteenth century, the Commons often tried to secure some redress of grievances before granting taxation. On very rare occasions, as in the so called "Good" parliament of 1376, when there was a general onslaught on the corrupt members of Edward III's household, they might even refuse a grant. This tactic, however, would hardly have worked in a parliament faced by a determined and active king, rather than by an obviously senile Edward III, who was patently in the hands of his courtiers. The furthest the Commons normally went was to claim that the grants sought could not really be necessary; and, very occasionally, in 1377 and 1404, to demand the appointment of "Treasurers at War" to ensure that the money voted was actually used for the extraordinary purposes for which it had been requested and not misapplied to ordinary expenditure. The grant of supply was not seen, as it came to be after 1689, as a means of political control. If the king needed the money, it was recognized in the Middle Ages that his subjects had a duty to supply it (Harriss 1975); as indeed it is accepted to be in the present very different times. In practice, parliament was seldom in itself much of a check on the king's will.

Very rarely, parliaments could force concessions from kings by delaying grants: in 1376, a determined body of commons was able to impeach and secure the conviction of prominent members of the royal household; in 1406, a parliament pressed for reforms in government for almost a year before securing some concessions. Even more rarely, a parliament might follow what was in effect a violent revolution, as in 1327, when Edward II was formally deposed after the revolt of 1326, and in 1388, when the "Merciless Parliament" condemned many of Richard II's favourites. In these cases, Parliament was in effect carrying through the objects of a revolution which had already occurred. But any control which seemed to be established scarcely outlasted the crises themselves. Edward III was certainly no less powerful than his father, despite the fact that the latter had been deposed; by 1389, Richard II had recovered effective authority, whatever the Merciless Parliament had done. These parliaments made little permanent difference to royal authority; those convicted in 1376 were mostly released and restored to favour after the parliament was dismissed. Treasurers at War acted for a time, both after 1377 and 1404, while the particular grants were being collected. But no parliament made the attempt to control the king permanently.

Hence, if any king failed to rule with the consent and support of his nobles and of the commons in parliament, there was an impasse, which neither side possessed any constitutional means to resolve. Discontented nobles had no resort short of open defiance or violent revolt. This was the only way in which a disenchanted baronage could attempt to bring pressure on a ruler to stop him doing whatever it was they objected to. This has often led to the medieval baronage being regarded as an unruly, violent and disorderly class. In reality, baronial revolts resulted from the lack of any other effective mechanism for protest.

It is important, however, to understand the nature of these revolts. They could be violent and sometimes, as in 1388, vindictive; but they were not usually attempts to remove the king. They were attempts to get him to change his ways, and, since changing one's ways is not easy, they seldom achieved very much in the long run. They resulted from a breakdown of relations, and they usually aimed to restore relations on better terms than had existed before.

Sometimes, of course, as in 1075 and 1173–74, they simply achieved nothing. The king proved too powerful and too well supported, and the only gain was simply that he might be a little more cautious in future. There is little the historian can detect to suggest that either William the Conqueror or Henry II actually did modify their behaviour.

There are examples of revolts which aimed at some kind of structural reform in government. The best instances were the revolts against Henry III (1258), Edward II (1310–11) and Richard II (1386). Each produced explicit proposals to establish a reformed government. In 1258 the object was to put the crown into commission, and subject it, at least for the time being, to baronial control since the rebels saw Henry III as personally incompetent. In 1310–11, Edward II was confronted with a written schedule of reforms, which he had to accept, a precedent which was followed by the parliament of 1386 in the reign of Richard II. In all these cases, the kings were left on the throne, though in 1386 very nominally. Deposition was not the immediate object.

As we have seen, however, none of these attempts succeeded in imposing a long-term political control. Each of these kings was able, for the time being at least, to escape from the restrictions imposed on them and recover effective power. In a crisis, a group of barons with support might take control, but the sense remained that the king was on the throne and had to be obeyed.

There was, however, one early occasion when the baronage contemplated actually removing the king – in 1216 when some were so outraged by John's failure to observe the "peace" enshrined in Magna Carta that they raised a revolt in favour of Prince Louis of France, the future King Louis VIII. It is pointless to speculate what might have happened if John had not conveniently died. In the event, there was little support for Louis against the infant Henry III; and this precedent seems to have been forgotten.

However, the depositions of Edward II and Richard II were not forgotten. Each, in his own way, had persisted in what the barons and others regarded as unacceptable behaviour. Edward II had suffered humiliating defeats both in Scotland and France. He had failed to abide by the reforms imposed under the Ordinances of 1311. He had allowed himself to be dominated by favourites, to the exclusion of nobles who regarded themselves as the king's "natural counsellors". Perhaps worst of all, he had allowed his last favourites, the Despensers, to mastermind a systematic programme of extortion, the proceeds of which he was incapable of using to save himself in the final crisis in 1326 (Fryde 1979). Richard II had proved himself self-willed and autocratic, not so much dominated by his favourites as elevating them to become the creatures of his personal policies. In 1397, when he retaliated against those who had carried through the revolt which culminated in the Merciless Parliament of 1388, his actions seemed to threaten the personal safety of his greatest subjects, while his confiscation of the Duchy of Lancaster implied a general threat to their lands and possessions. The depositions of Edward and Richard created constitutional precedents which were to be much in mind in the times of the Wars of the Roses, and were to be quoted, for example, by Warwick and Clarence in their 1469 manifesto, issued in Calais before the campaign which culminated in the battle of Edgecote (Dockray 1988: 68–73, especially at p. 69). Deposition had emerged as the ultimate, if not very satisfactory, sanction which could be brought against an errant king.

The deposition of Edward II was a limited step: The king was declared "incorrigible without hope of amendment" (Chrimes and Brown 1961, 37–8) and formally deposed as incapable of government. He was replaced, nominally at least, by his rightful heir, the young prince who was to become Edward III. This did not disturb the royal line, and might seem a very reasonable way of dealing with a king who was regarded as hopelessly incompetent, even if it involved a violent revolution and the elimination of some of his hated servants. The precedent, of course, was not forgotten. No-one had occasion, so far as we know, to remind Edward III of it, though he too had his difficulties, for instance in 1341, 1371 and 1376. But the events of 1327 haunted Richard II's reign.

Relations between Richard and many of his leading nobles reached a crisis in 1386 when the opposition formally attacked the chancellor, Michael de la Pole. This was, in fact, a way of attacking the young king himself, who had assumed personal authority in

1382 at the age of 16. The "reforms" finally imposed on Richard after a stormy session effectively placed the government in commission in order to overhaul the whole working, of both the royal household and the government. In the course of these disputes, according to the account of Henry Knighton, Richard had withdrawn to Eltham palace, apparently to avoid demands for the dismissal of the chancellor. There he was confronted by a formal parliamentary delegation, consisting of his uncle Thomas of Woodstock and Thomas Arundel, then Bishop of Ely, later Archbishop of Canterbury. After some fruitless argument, they cited an alleged "statute", which, they said, "had been put in force no long time ago", that if the king, by ill-counsel or contumacy alienated himself from his people and would not govern by the laws or the counsel of his nobles, then "it was lawful ... to depose the king from his throne and raise to the throne another near member of the royal line" (Chrimes and Brown 1961: 132, quoting the *Chronicon Henrici Knighton*). This was a clear and explicit reference to the deposition of Edward II, which inevitably was becoming part of constitutional precedent.

Richard was forced to return to parliament, and Michael de la Pole was impeached. A commission of 12 was to take over the government for a year. Richard however spent the time preparing a counter-coup. The leaders of the opposition, in an attempt to protect themselves, "appealed" a lengthy list of Richard's advisers and supporters (i.e. brought formal accusations against them which came eventually before parliament in 1388, hence Richard's opponents are known as the "appellants"). The result of these appeals was open war, in which Richard's forces were routed. His chief supporters were then condemned, and some executed, in the Merciless Parliament which followed. Despite this setback, Richard was able to recover authority in 1389, and, after ruling cautiously for eight years, felt in a position to take his revenge for the events of 1388. The leading appellants of 1388 were condemned in the parliament of 1397. That revenge and the exile of John of Gaunt's son, Henry Bolingbroke, followed by the confiscation of the Duchy of Lancaster after Gaunt's death in 1399, provoked the revolution of 1399, in which Bolingbroke seized the throne.

What actually happened in 1399 brought the possibility of the Wars of the Roses significantly nearer. We do not know whom

Gloucester and Bishop Arundel had in mind in making their threat in 1386 to replace Richard by another member of the royal line. It has been suggested that, by December 1387, the idea of deposing Richard had gone further, but that it came to nothing because there was no agreement as to which member of the royal family should succeed the childless Richard (Clarke 1937: 91–95). In 1399, that problem was solved by the initiative of Henry Bolingbroke, who, after a carefully orchestrated claim, became Henry IV. But his right was not unchallengeable. Although Edward III had been the unquestionable heir of Edward II, Bolingbroke was not the unquestionable heir of Richard II: the descendants of Lionel Duke of Clarence, second surviving son of Edward III, surely had in law a better claim than those of John of Gaunt, the third son. That meant the line of March, ultimately York, even though the line went through a woman, Philippa, Lionel's daughter, and was in 1399 represented by a minor. These events in 1399 set a further and damning precedent: from then on, should a king be regarded as incapable or perverse, anyone with a colourable claim to the throne could put it forward. Because several noble lines were descended from Edward III, it was not difficult to find claimants.

This did not mean that 1399 made the Wars of the Roses inevitable. Had the Lancastrian dynasty remained competent and effective, it might well have survived. Even Henry VI remained on the throne for 23 years after he came of age in 1437. But reluctant as his nobles were to remove him, even as late as the autumn of 1460, when York tried formally to claim the throne, the precedent of 1399 made such action conceivable. Alternative lines could claim that the throne was theirs by right. This had added another factor to the circumstances which made the Wars of the Roses possible.

CHAPTER 5

Failings of government

In fact, the immediate cause of disaster lay with the kings and their advisers. Henry VI, Edward IV in his first reign, and Richard III all acted in ways which seriously disturbed the society of the late Middle Ages, and which the political structures of that era could not correct. Their weaknesses were different from each other, but all contributed by their actions to a collapse of the system, though the difficulties of Edward IV in his first reign stemmed as much from the excessive expectations of Warwick and Clarence as from Edward's own failings.

The personal government of Henry VI

As we have seen in Chapter 2, when Henry VI was declared of age in 1437, just before his 16th birthday, he entered on a difficult inheritance. Henry's own desire for peace was at odds with the strong feelings of many of his barons, who lamented the sad decline from the triumphs of his father, Henry V. It would have taken a very able king to achieve either victory or an effective peace in such a fraught situation.

Henry proved indecisive and subject to pressure. Any progress in negotiations with France required that he should at least give up the use of the title of King of France, as Edward III had done for a period after the Treaty of Brétigny/Calais in 1360. Under the influence of Gloucester, and to the despair of the negotiators in France, Henry refused, and negotiations collapsed in 1439. Henry's government then pursued a mixture of peace negotiations and warlike demonstrations, until the ultimate disasters of 1450 and 1453. Henry's desire for peace, and his marriage to Margaret of Anjou, which eventually led him to the surrender of Maine in 1448, had alienated the supporters of war. His occasional permission for or even encouragement of aggressive tactics confused the situation. In 1449, for example, François de Surienne, an Arragonese captain long in the service of Henry VI, recently rewarded by election to the Order of the Garter, led an attack which temporarily captured the Breton *bastide* of Fougères, in what appears to have been an attempt to strengthen English influence in Brittany against the French. Despite the rapid disavowal of de Surienne by Henry VI and his council, there is little doubt that this escapade had been planned with their full knowledge and consent (Griffiths 1981: 509–13). The natural consequence was to provoke the French King Charles VII without seriously obstructing his offensives. As we have seen, the disasters in war contributed very significantly to the explosion against Henry's government in 1450. Henry himself must bear a good deal of the responsibility for what happened.

Henry also showed weakness in his management of government at home. His councillors quickly noticed with alarm a tendency in the young king to respond generously to any request made to him, without any attempt to investigate or consider the consequences. As early as 1438, the clerk of the Council had to advise Henry to be more cautious about granting pardons, offices and lands: this followed several instances of Henry's acting without consultation or consideration, culminating in his sale of the strategically and financially important lordship and castle of Chirk on the Welsh march to Cardinal Beaufort. Three years later, however, he was giving royal favours to the Earl of Devon, without any regard for the fact that Devon was engaged in a violent dispute with Lord Bonville, which the Council was desperately trying to resolve (Wolffe 1981: 106–7).

As time went on, Henry's blend of obstinacy and easygoing benevolence was to prove disastrous. He was easily led by those with whom he was in contact, and unwilling to listen to criticism. This gave enormous influence to the members of his household, which they were too ready to use to their own advantage. It was the classic problem of the influence of favourites, too able to influence the crown, and so excluding others from the benefits of royal favour. From the start of Henry's personal rule, it became obvious that the members of the household were the channel to favours and grants; and also that they could pursue their own interests with impunity. This gave them power to tyrannize the localities where they held lands and could secure offices. William de la Pole. who inherited the earldom of Suffolk, became Steward of the Household, its effective head, in 1433, marquess in 1444 and duke in 1448. He became steward of the Chiltern Hundreds, constable of Wallingford castle, steward of the honours of Wallingford and St Valéry, chief justice of Chester, Flint and North Wales, chief steward of the northern parts of the Duchy of Lancaster, and steward and surveyor of all mines in England and Wales. On top of this he received a long list of manors from the crown lands (Wolffe 1981: 111–2). Lesser members of the Household also got their share (ibid. 109, 112–3).

But it was the power to abuse justice in the localities that did the most damage. The best evidence for this comes from Kent and East Anglia: the first as a result of the documentation centring on Jack Cade's rebellion in 1450; the second in the voluminous pages of the *Paston Letters*. As the evidence of aggrieved parties, neither source is entirely impartial, but there are too many examples of corruption for it to be ignored.

In Kent, the trouble centred on James Fiennes, a long-standing ally of Suffolk and a member of an important Sussex family whose main seat was at Herstmonceux, overlooking the Pevensey levels. As an esquire of the household, attending personally on the king, he had built up his own empire throughout the south-east with royal grants in Kent and Surrey. He was at various times sheriff of Surrey and Sussex, and constable of Rochester castle. He also became steward of the Sussex and Kentish lands of the deceased Earl of Warwick, chamberlain of the king's household by 1447, and constable of Dover. He gained the title of Lord Saye and Sele and a place in the Council, and in 1449 the office of Lord Treasurer. With him, there rose other lesser men: Stephen Slegge became undersheriff of Kent, escheator, sheriff in 1448–49 and MP for Dover in 1449; William Crowmer, son of a London Alderman, was sheriff of Kent in 1444–45 and again in 1449; William Isle was regularly on the Commission of the Peace for Kent, and sheriff in 1446–47; and Robert Est was the keeper of Maidstone gaol. This group monopolized all the positions of power in the county, and their extortions, false imprisonments, and violent outrages were to be listed in considerable detail in the complaints and later indictments thrown up in and after Jack Cade's rebellion (Harvey 1991: 36–42).

In East Anglia, the trouble centred on the misdeeds of another group of household men, likewise followers of Suffolk: Thomas Tuddenham, for a time Keeper of the Great Wardrobe, John Heydon, John Ulveston, and Thomas Daniel. Tuddenham acted as steward of Suffolk's manor of Swaffham, some 15 miles north of Thetford, which brought him near to Paston country, and so to special notoriety. This also happened to John Heydon of Baconsthorp, even closer to the Pastons (Wolffe 1981: 122). While Suffolk ruled, these men were unchallengeable, and abuses multiplied: among the Paston manuscripts in the British Library there is a list of complaints against Tuddenham and Heydon which include cases of false imprisonment, thefts and false indictments by their followers, maintenance of alleged wrongdoers by Tuddenham himself, and violence and extortion committed by him against the Prior of West Acre, a wealthy Augustinian house near Castle Acre in West Norfolk (see Gairdner 1904: 175, ii: 213–16). After Suffolk's fall, proceedings could be taken. Complainants even secured a judgement against Tuddenham and Heydon in the latter part of 1450. But influence still worked, and by May 1451, the two seemed restored to favour under the influence of the new favourite, the Duke of Somerset (Griffiths 1981: 588–91).

Such widespread abuses aroused frustration and fury, which was revealed in the impeachment of Suffolk in 1450, in his murder when Henry VI tried to save him by exile, and in the outbreak of Jack Cade's rebellion. The manifestoes issued by the rebels emphasized both the failures in France and the corruption at home, as well as the complete financial collapse of Henry's government; and these same points were taken up by the Duke of York in his campaign later in the summer when he tried to remove what he regarded as Henry's incompetent and corrupt advisers.

The breakdown in finances was not wholly Henry's fault. No medieval English king really possessed regular revenues adequate to his responsibilities, yet parliament constantly expected that kings would "live of their own", and regularly tried to limit taxation to defined "extraordinary" expenditure. In practice, under whatever excuses, taxation was fairly regular, and most kings had to depend on this; but parliament's tendency was to make as small grants as possible and often to delay making them until the situation was serious. This was particularly likely to happen when things were going badly, as they were in the 1440s. By the late 1440s, Henry's need for money was desperate; yet in 1445 parliament made a niggardly grant in its first session, and nothing at all in the next two. By 1449, in the words of Professor Griffiths, "the Lancastrian régime was well and truly bankrupt" (Griffiths 1981: 376–94).

Whether York would have done any better is uncertain: twice, during Henry's periods of incapacity, he became Protector, but had little chance to achieve anything. Essentially, the 1450s saw a prolonged struggle between York and his supporters against the "court party", headed first by Somerset, and then after his death at St Albans, by the queen, Margaret of Anjou. It was a struggle which was only ended in the upheavals of 1460–61, in which York himself was killed and his son, Edward IV, won the throne.

In the years of his personal government from 1437 till his illness in 1453, Henry VI had proved incapable of managing government effectively; and the result was not only financial collapse, but also a breakdown of order and bitter faction fighting between the courtiers, headed ultimately by the queen on one side, and discontented nobles, frustrated by the corruption and the incompetence of those around the king, on the other.

The first reign of Edward IV, 1461–70

The young earl of March, who became the first Yorkist king as Edward IV in 1461, seemed a total contrast to Henry VI. Apparently undismayed by his father's death at the battle of Wakefield and Queen Margaret's victory over Warwick at the second battle of St Albans, he was able, as we have seen, to seize the throne, and almost wipe out the Lancastrian party at the bloody and decisive battle of Towton at the end of March 1461. Thereafter the Lancastrian cause was confined to ineffective plots and a rather more serious rearguard action in the north, which lasted till its decisive defeat at Hexham in 1464. From that time, Edward IV seemed secure and unchallenged. Yet in 1469–70, as we have seen in pp. 27–30, he was unseated and driven into exile. What had gone wrong?

In part, it was the inevitable difficulties facing any usurper. His obligations to those who have helped him to the throne create problems once he is king. If he rewards them as they expect, he arouses hostility in others; if he does not, he provokes those who had been his staunchest supporters. Kingmakers often turn rebels, as Henry IV found when the Percies, who had backed his coup in 1399, were in revolt by 1403. The revolt by Warwick in 1469 followed the same pattern.

Edward had indeed rewarded Warwick handsomely for his support. Not only was he made Great Chamberlain of England, an honorific office, and was confirmed as captain of Calais, a title he had been given originally under Henry VI, but he was also made constable of Dover, warden of the Cinque ports, and steward of the Duchy of Lancaster honours in Lancashire and Cheshire, and Duchy honours in Yorkshire and in the Midlands, to list only the greatest of his rewards. Warwick had no reason at all to complain of Edward's generosity; indeed he continued to serve him well, both in the prolonged campaigns against the surviving Lancastrians in the north and in diplomatic missions, particularly to France. There, Warwick built up a useful rapport with the new French king, Louis XI, who succeeded to the throne in 1461. Now that there was only Calais left of the English lands in France, a rapprochement with the French monarchy was sensible policy, and Warwick worked hard for this.

Yet Edward, who took the throne only some six weeks before his nineteenth birthday, was hardly likely to let Warwick dominate him permanently. Quite soon, there were signs that he was developing policies of his own. In two areas where he had first seemed to give authority to Warwick, he rapidly entrusted power to others. In south Wales, where he had given the title to powerful lordships to Warwick, he then very quickly gave actual control of them to William Herbert; while in the Midlands, he balanced Warwick's grant of Tutbury with the grant to William Hastings of the Duchy honour of Leicester, a grant which established in a commanding position in the centre of England one who rapidly became Edward's close associate (Ross 1974: 70–1). Such actions betokened a move by Edward to build up his own supporters in positions of power; they also indicated at least the possibility from the start of a rift with Warwick. It was a possibility that developed as Edward, now in his early twenties, went more and more his own way.

One of his problems was to hold on to and reward those who had helped towards his victory while at the same time winning over all he could of the remaining Lancastrians. His efforts at this last were not always successful. For example, he extended mercy repeatedly to the young Duke of Somerset, the son of the duke killed fighting on the Lancastrian side at the first battle of St Albans in 1455, but Somerset as often deserted again to the Lancastrian side, and was ultimately executed after the battle of Hexham in 1464. With many others, however, Edward was successful. Yet his policy of reconciliation caused some tension with those who had fought for him at Towton, who naturally expected and received the lion's share of the pickings. It was not an easy path to tread.

Nevertheless Warwick continued to work hard for Edward and to suffer further rebuffs. Indeed, he probably felt that in the north he and his brother Montague were fighting battles for Edward, in which the king himself showed little interest. Nor did Warwick's diplomatic efforts find favour. His efforts to arrange a French marriage for Edward collapsed when Edward himself married Elizabeth Woodville in secret and without the knowledge of any of his counsellors. This marriage might indeed be regarded as the culmination of Edward's attempts to win over former Lancastrians, though no surviving contemporary or near contemporary commentator regarded it in that light. On the other hand, it caused serious political problems. Such a marriage to a subject had no precedent in England since the Norman Conquest, and the existence of a group of step-children and other relatives for the king created difficulties. It changed the nature of Edward's court, since the queen's relatives inevitably gained from her advancement, and became one of the dominant groups around the king. Her father became, in due course, Earl Rivers and Treasurer of England. Many of her family secured advantageous marriages: her brother married the dowager duchess of Norfolk; sisters married the heirs of the duke of Buckingham, the earl of Essex, and the earl of Kent, and the son of Edward's very prominent supporter, William Lord Herbert, while the queen's son by her first marriage married the heiress of the duchess of Exeter. These marriages were probably regarded by the families concerned as a good investment, providing as they did useful contacts with a rising group at court. On the other hand, though the Woodville family gained great influence at court, they did not displace the others, such as Hastings and Herbert, who had early emerged as Edward's closest political associates. Nor, for all their influence at court, did they receive direct grants from the crown on anything like the scale that Warwick, Hastings or Herbert had done in the early days of Edward's reign (Ross 1974: 92–6). Edward was clearly attempting to strike a balance between his various supporters, though it was not necessarily a balance that was appreciated by Warwick. It is hard to be sure how widely the advancement of the Woodvilles was resented. Warwick laid great stress on it in his propaganda in 1469, and at least one chronicler, the anonymous writer usually mis-labelled as William of Worcester, also stressed the series of Wood-ville marriages and their unpopularity with Warwick and other nobles. But it remains difficult to separate propaganda from fact in this matter.

Edward certainly provoked Warwick over his marriage and its consequences. He made matters worse by the line he then pursued in foreign policy, where he increasingly sought contacts and good relations with Burgundy. This policy made good sense, in view of the importance of English trade with the Low Countries. Unfortu-nately, Charles the Bold, the expectant heir to the elderly duke of Burgundy, Philip the Good, was on bad terms with Louis XI of France. Warwick, however, as we have seen, continued to work for an alliance with France. Edward, in this tricky situation, handled negotiations in a way almost calculated to enrage Warwick. In 1466 and 1467, it seems clear that Warwick was conducting what Edward regarded as purely formal negotiations with France, while negotiations with Burgundy, which Edward regarded as critical, were being handled by others, members of the Woodville family among them. In the end, the crucial decision in 1467, the agreement by which Edward's sister Margaret was to marry Charles the Bold, was reached while Warwick was kept occupied with an embassy to France where Edward did not intend to achieve anything. Warwick was clearly offended. He retired to his estates after the agreement with Burgundy, and it was only with difficulty that he seemed for the time to have been placated. Even so, it was not till 1469 that Warwick actually launched his revolt. He perhaps considered that he had been remarkably long-suffering in accepting the way that Edward had for years been going his own way; his ultimate revolt seems a result of pique at what he took to be a series of rebuffs for his work and the policies he supported.

The support for Warwick's rebellion of Edward's own brother, George Duke of Clarence, is more difficult to explain, except in terms of his demonstrably unstable character. Clarence might of course have hoped to retain a position as Edward's heir presumptive; but given Edward's marriage and his recorded paternity within and outside marriage, this was surely implausible. The position of a king's brother is notoriously difficult, for he enjoys high rank and yet has no clear expectations. Clarence was obviously concerned to find a secure status – reports of plans for a Burgundian marriage were current in the 1460s – but any such project was blocked by Edward who did not want Clarence to establish himself abroad, as might have followed from such a marriage.

Warwick's propaganda in 1469 alleged that Edward had fallen under the influence of "certain seditious persons" and tried to compare him with Edward II, Richard II and Henry VI, the previous kings who had been deposed for favouritism and misgovernment (Dockray 1988: 68–9). This was far from fair. Edward had established effective rule, suppressed disorder and was pursuing a defensible foreign policy. Yet he had contributed by his actions to his troubles. His marriage had been improvident; he had allowed his court to be dominated by the queen's relatives, and his handling of relations with France, in which Warwick was so much involved, had in two periods, over his own marriage and over the marriage treaty with Burgundy in 1467, been much less than straightforward. In other ways, too, he had failed to satisfy the expectations of his supporters. One chronicler, John Warkworth, writing probably towards the end of Edward's reign, but speaking specifically of the 1460s said:

> when King Edward reigned, the people looked after all the aforesaid prosperity and peace, but it came not; but one battle after another [referring to the fighting in the north in the early 1460s], and much

trouble and great loss of goods among the common people; as first the 15th of all their goods, and then a whole 15th [a reference to Edward IV's taxation] (Dockray 1988: 34).

Edward had certainly shown himself more capable that Henry VI; but some discontent evidently remained.

Yet that discontent hardly ran very deep. By harping on Edward's "evil advisers" in their manifesto of 1469, Warwick and Clarence gained some support. There was no obvious hostile reaction to the removal of the Woodvilles and other favourites; yet, on the other hand, there was no enthusiasm for a government patently headed by Warwick. He was able to do nothing effective and had soon to release Edward from constraint. In 1470, Edward had no difficulty in crushing the Lincolnshire rebellion; and Warwick and Clarence could only flee into exile. Their triumph on their return in the summer of 1471 is hard to explain: the collapse of Edward's resistance seems to stem from his own miscalculation when he was expecting help from Montague which was not forthcoming. It does not appear to betoken any general support for the restoration of Henry VI. When Edward returned in 1471, his position proved eventually strong after a hesitant start. In the end, Warwick could not capitalize on such discontent as there was against Edward IV; and even Clarence deserted him.

After the victories of Barnet and Tewkesbury and the crushing of the final effort of Fauconberg's rebellion, Edward's authority was restored. The combination of dissident Yorkists and surviving Lancastrians had seemed for a short time powerful, but they hardly represented deep-seated discontent. Now that the leaders of rebellion were removed, Edward's position proved strong enough. When, in 1478, he ultimately lost patience with his brother Clarence and had him executed, this may, as Polydore Vergil suggested, have left the king emotionally distressed (Ellis 1844: 168) but it did not disturb his authority (see Pronay and Cox 1986: 146–7).

The remainder of Edward's reign showed that he was able to overcome many of the problems which beset Henry VI. Finance had been one of Henry's greatest weaknesses: Edward IV improved the situation partly by doing all he could to encourage trade and so enhance his customs revenue; also by making determined efforts to improve the administration of royal lands, mainly by bringing them and their revenues under the direct control of his officials, where previously they had largely been farmed out by the Exchequer; and by gaining pensions from France in return for abandoning an attempt to revive the French war in 1475 (see Ross 1974, Chapter 16 and especially pp. 379–87). His grasp over the kingdom was strengthened by the development of regional lordships, especially in Wales and the north. There was a good deal of experimentation in working these out: already in his first reign he had made use of Herbert for a time as his chief agent in Wales. In his second reign, Edward was able to rely more closely for control of the regions on his brother Richard and the queen's relatives. particularly her brother Anthony, the second Earl Rivers, who appears to have been widely admired, and is remembered as a patron of the printer Caxton. In Wales, he used the council which he established around his infant son, the future Edward V, at Ludlow, a council which was headed by Earl Rivers; while in the north he relied on the great lordship which he created for his brother Richard, who established an effective working relationship with the chief local magnate, Percy Earl of Northumberland. In the southern parts of England, Edward kept a closer control himself, often relying on members of his household who held lands in the area (Ross 1974: 199–203, 334–9; Horrox 1989: 49–58). It proved an effective system while it was staffed by people he could trust, and it provided models and some warnings for the Tudors in their handling of these problems, as did more general aspects of Edward's government.

The troubles of Richard III

The troubles which came over the Yorkist dynasty in 1483–85 were created by Richard of Gloucester. As Thomas More said in his *Life of King Richard III*, when Edward IV died, his throne was secure, his country at peace, and no disturbance to be expected (see Sylvester 1963). To More, the reign of Richard III was an unhappy contrast to the security enjoyed under his brother.

Richard's troubles stemmed directly from his usurpation. We shall never know exactly what brought him to the path he took. His career so far had shown high ability; he had conducted himself well in difficult situations, and acted as the loyal and very effective supporter of his brother's government in the north and elsewhere. He had won the respect of those who worked with him, and more than their respect. The citizens of York went out of their way after Bosworth to record their regard for him and their sorrow for his death, at a time when such expressions might have seemed unnecessary, even dangerous. From the time of his service to Edward IV, he gained adherents and an affinity, some of whom at least fought and died for him at Bosworth.

The waters have been so muddied by later writers, either producing Tudor propaganda, or more commonly using Richard as a dire warning of the consequences of political ambition, that it is now impossible fully to understand the significance of events in the crucial weeks of May and June 1483. What we can see are the consequences.

Richard's usurpation, and still more the rumours of the death of the princes, shattered the Yorkist party which had seemed so secure under Edward IV. Many of the loyal household servants of King Edward, and some even of the long-standing affinity of Richard of Gloucester, joined in the rising in the autumn of 1483. Since it collapsed so quickly, it is hard to tell exactly its nature, or to be certain of its aims. According to the Croyland Chronicle, it began as a movement to rescue the princes, and then gathered force as rumours spread of their death. It was at that stage that those who were finally alienated from Richard III had perforce to turn to Henry Earl of Richmond, almost the last surviving Lancastrian claimant, and until this point scarcely heard of in history. But most of those whom we know to have been involved in the rebellion were in no sense Lancastrians. The list of those subsequently attainted by Richard III includes most of the surviving Woodvilles except Queen Elizabeth and her daughters, and many of the Kentish gentry who had been prominent in the court of Edward IV. It was essentially a rising of the courtiers of Edward IV against the usurper Richard (Ross 1981: 105–12). It was Richmond himself and his relatively small group of fellow exiles who might have contributed the only Lancastrian elements, had they arrived in England in time to join in. Richmond's army at Bosworth in 1485, which did include those, such as Jasper Tudor, who had shared his exile from the first, also included a goodly number of the rebels of 1483 who had escaped to join him in Brittany, and to accompany his later move to France. Men such as Giles Daubeny and Richard Guildford, former servants of Edward IV and leaders in the rebellion of 1483, were to gain prominence as servants of Henry VII; his standard bearer, killed at Bosworth, was apparently the William Brandon who figures in the list of Kentish rebels in 1483, rather than his father, Sir William, who also revolted against Richard, though not till 1484. Richard was defeated at Bosworth by an army which contained many previously ultra-loyal Yorkists, who had been decisively alienated by his accession, and by the presumed deaths of the princes.

The evidence is that Richard became well aware of this reaction. In the weeks after his coronation, on his apparently triumphal progress through the country, he seemed to be well established. He was welcomed by the towns he visited; and responded graciously, often declining their gifts of money. But Buckingham's Rebellion revealed that too many of Edward IV's most loyal servants had been alienated. In the south of England, it seems that thereafter there were few he felt he could trust. He had more confidence in some of his northern followers, and it was to them he often turned to fill the gaps left by those who had fled, or would not serve him. A king depended on loyal service throughout his realm; Richard's base of service contracted sharply, and he had to press those he trusted to serve him ever more intensively, and at times beyond what they could manage (see Horrox 1989, Chapters 4, 6). Towards the end of 1484, Richard was faced with a crisis in the Pale of Calais, when James Blount, the commander of the castle of Hammes, deserted to Richmond along with the earl of Oxford, who had been imprisoned there since 1473. Richard's only solution was to make one of his most trusted supporters, James Tyrell, lieutenant of Guisnes, and after six months' delay another, Thomas Whortley, commander of Hammes. This removed men who had been crucial in maintaining Richard's authority in Wales and in the forfeited estates of the duke of Buckingham in the Midlands. Tyrell was left still notionally representing Richard in Wales, despite the fact that he was actually abroad (Ross 1981: 202 n.28; Horrox 1989: 290–1). At Bosworth itself, the Stanleys deserted him, and the earl of Northumberland may also have acted cautiously, waiting to see the outcome. His troops were certainly not engaged, but analysts differ as to whether this was Northumberland's choice, or whether the terrain of the battlefield prevented his troops coming to grips. Dr Horrox's study shows that these were only the most prominent of many who hesitated to support Richard.

Conclusion

This analysis has argued that the essential causes of the political collapse of the mid-fifteenth century lay in the various failings and actions of the kings themselves. Henry VI proved incapable, and the result of a collapse of authority was disturbance and intermittent civil war which lasted for some six years. Edward IV was far more capable; but he in turn contributed to the temporary breakdown of 1469–71; on the other hand, Warwick and Clarence, by their petulance and blatant self-interest, contributed much more than did Edward, and their solution, the restoration of Henry VI, was hardly acceptable. Richard III's usurpation, by shattering the Yorkist polity which had existed since 1471, provoked a new period of instability, which was not necessarily concluded by his death in 1485. Henry VII had still to prove himself, and it was some years before he was secure.

How far should one call the whole period The Wars of the Roses? Henry VI's failings did indeed provoke a dynastic struggle, which lasted till 1461. But the later troubles were not essentially dynastic. What have been called The Years of Crisis in Edward IV's reign, 1469–1471, were not in essence a conflict between Lancaster and York. They were a reaction of dissident Yorkists against the court which had gathered round Edward IV. Warwick tried first to regain control of the still young king; only when that failed was he finally driven to revert to the Lancastrian Henry VI. Barnet and Tewkesbury ended any Lancastrian threat. Richard III in his turn provoked what was essentially a Yorkist backlash, rather than a Lancastrian revival, by his usurpation and the rumoured murder of the princes. The Wars of the Roses is a very inadequate label for a complex and intensely disturbed period.

Epilogue: the Tudor solution

In the long run, Tudor propaganda was to emphasize and reiterate the claim that the Wars of the Roses were ended in 1486 by the marriage of Henry VII and Elizabeth of York. This was grossly to oversimplify both the causes and the resolution of the troubles which wracked England from 1450 till 1485. Indeed, in the most obvious sense, the problems were not solved in 1485. Not until the executions of the Earl of Warwick and Perkin Warbeck in 1499 was Henry regarded as sufficiently secure on the throne to be an acceptable father-in-law for the daughter of Ferdinand and Isabella of Spain. Further, as we have seen, the problems of the mid-fifteenth century were not simply, or even primarily, dynastic. They were problems of political power and political management, and they had to be solved in those terms. The marriage of Lancaster and York was a useful public proclamation of Henry's intention to restore unity; but he and his dynasty had to solve more fundamental problems if they were to survive.

Since the outbreaks of violence mostly resulted from either general incapacity, in the case of Henry VI, or particular errors of judgement by Edward IV and Richard III, the first essential was to avoid such weaknesses. Henry VII, Henry VIII and Elizabeth I were all forceful and capable personalities, and they thus achieved the first essential of effective kingship. But the "mid-Tudor crisis" showed that even Tudor monarchs might face a recurrence of what looked very like former troubles. Throughout the century, official proclamations and political literature constantly returned to the importance of order, the dangers of treason, and the awful perils of "vaulting ambition". Shakespeare's *Richard III* ends with a plea to

"Abate the edge of traitors, gracious Lord, that would reduce these bloody days again"; the *exempla* in the *Mirror for Magistrates*, almost all taken from the fifteenth century, warn of the dreadful consequences of treasonable political ambition. The vital importance of a strong monarchy is still stressed in the imagery surrounding Queen Elizabeth. The Rainbow Portrait at Hatfield House, for instance, has the inscription *"Non sine Sole Iris"*: "No Rainbow without the Sun", saying in effect "No Peace without Elizabeth", since the rainbow is a symbol of peace, and the sun of the Queen. The emphasis on these themes suggests a sense of insecurity underlying the apparent triumphalism of the Tudor state.

One evident need of a successful ruler was secure finance. Henry VI had demonstrated the consequences of lack of money and financial improvidence, and it was a lesson grasped not only by Henry VII and his successors, but also very clearly by Edward IV (Ross 1974, Chapter 16). Indeed it is a commonplace that Henry VII's financial measures to improve financial administration were very much a continuation and development of those of Edward IV.

But more was needed than improved administration. A fundamental weakness in Henry VI's position was the lack of a secure landed base for the monarchy, important not only for revenue but for the local influence that came with lands in the direct control of the king. Henry IV and Henry V had had something of the kind in the lands of the Duchy of Lancaster; Henry VI's generosity had gravely weakened his position, as Chief Justice John Fortescue had pointed out in his *Governance of England* (Plummer 1885). Edward IV began to expand the royal demesnes, a process continued by Henry VII and dramatically followed up by Henry VIII in his dissolution of the monasteries, which tripled the crown's income from land, at least in the immediate aftermath of the dissolution (Gunn 1995: 24–8). This gave a solid basis for royal government which had been lacking to Henry VI.

The fundamental need, however, as much for the Tudors as for their predecessors, was the capacity to manage their landed magnates. There is a prevalent myth that the Wars of the Roses destroyed the power of the over-mighty subjects. They did no such thing. Death-rates were high during the periods of conflict, but overall it does not appear that the landed classes were destroyed. Heirs survived and in due course succeeded. John Howard, Duke of

Norfolk, died at Bosworth, but his son, Thomas Howard Earl of Surrey, recovered the title in 1514 after his victory at Flodden. England under the Tudors was as much a country of landed magnates as it had been in the fifteenth century. Some were "new" men, some members of houses of longer standing, but that was no different from the situation in any previous period. As far back as we know of it, the nobility had changed composition by new elevations, often by marriage to heiresses, to replace natural extinction. It does not seem that the rate of change in the fifteenth century was noticeably greater than at any other period. What mattered was whether the sovereign could retain the loyalty of the magnates.

This, even in the awkward years of the mid-century, the Tudors succeeded in doing. Rebellions certainly occurred, but their thrones were seldom in danger. Northumberland's attempt to exclude Mary in 1553 only revealed the essential loyalty to the dynasty. In part this was a result of the sagacity and determination of the rulers themselves, but they also owed much to the capacity of their servants. The structures of government were certainly changing in the sixteenth century, however one defines the Tudor Revolution in Government. One new feature was the remarkable prominence of a series of royal servants, from Empson and Dudley through Wolsey and Cromwell, to Lord Burghley and his son Robert Cecil. These men perhaps contributed as much as Henry VII, Henry VIII and Elizabeth I to the management of the Tudor polity. The changes which made their influence possible certainly helped to solve the problems of political management, by making it less totally dependent on the capability of the sovereign him or herself. But these servants could only do what their ruler permitted. In the end, everything depended on the good sense of the king or queen, as the ultimate fate of Charles I demonstrated.

However, there were things that helped the rulers of the sixteenth century to be more successful than their predecessors. Not all their advantages were of their own making.

One factor in destabilizing the fifteenth century had certainly been the Hundred Years' War, which could not be won, and yet could hardly be laid aside. This was a very important aspect of the predicament of Henry VI; and one which both Edward IV and Henry VII were careful not to reactivate. Both actually embarked on expeditions in France, in 1475 and 1492 respectively; however, both treated these expeditions as means to extract a profitable peace, and made no serious attempt to revive the war. Henry VIII, it should be said, was less circumspect. Both in France and Scotland, he had grandiose ambitions which, since they were unrealistic, might easily have destabilized his position at home; the expense they caused and the humiliations that ensued certainly made things more difficult for his successors.

Many developments helped the Tudors to contain the power of the magnates. One, whether deliberate or not, was the emergence of a royal court as a focus for the ambitions of the nobility. Medieval nobles were essentially creatures of their estates. They lived on them and their power depended on their influence over the localities where their estates were concentrated. They might attend the king on formal occasions, but they were not regularly present at court and they did not wish to be. Indeed, historians of the Middle Ages refer rather to the *royal household* than to the royal *court*. Athough the court is essentially a more magnificent and ceremonial royal household, it is, in its new form, a development in England of the early sixteenth century (Starkey et al. 1987). As such it served to attract the great nobles into the royal circle and attach them to the crown. Place at court was highly valued; it was the source of royal favour and advancement, and dismissal from court was a dreaded punishment. It gave the sovereign a personal influence over his nobles which earlier rulers had not had.

The greatest element in binding the nobles' loyalty to the crown was self-interest, and in the age of the Reformation, the crown had enormous capacity to extend favour. The successive dissolutions of religious orders in the later 1530s brought to the crown enormous landed wealth. These orders owned something like a third of the land of England; and Henry was keen to sell this off to raise immediate cash. Hence, the early sixteenth century has been called the Age of Plunder (Hoskins 1976) and the access to that plunder in the 1530s and 40s lay in the court. The *Lisle Letters*, a sixteenth century collection as valuable in its way as the *Paston Letters* for the fifteenth, are a wonderful revelation of the workings of the Tudor state (Byrne 1981). There we see the search for pickings; for monastic lands everywhere, and for prime urban sites, especially the sites of friaries in London; the suits to those of influence at Court, above all to Cromwell; and the utter shamelessness with which the pickings were pursued. With so much at stake, everything depended on access to court. Only the utterly rejected could contemplate rebellion, or even stepping out of line. The profits of the dissolution of the monasteries were a most potent element in holding together the Tudor state. It was a temporary effect, but its consequences were to last well on in the century.

The success of the Tudors was as complex a phenomenon as the failure of Lancastrians and Yorkists. It was certainly not simply a consequence of binding up dynastic quarrels; there was far more to it than even the succession of several able and personally dominant sovereigns. Even the reign of Elizabeth was marked by rebellions, plots, threats to the sovereign's life, countered by elaborate sworn alliances of loyal nobles, aimed at her preservation. Yet, for all the Elizabethan obsession with the troubles of the fifteenth century, the world had changed dramatically in the hundred years after the battle of Bosworth. The ultimate danger now was foreign invasion by Spain in the interest of Catholicism. Internal plots, such as those on behalf of Mary Queen of Scots, were mainly serious in that context, but it was possible to hold the nation behind the crown, as Elizabeth did, by calling for unity in face of foreign threats. This is explicit in the final speech of Shakespeare's *King John*, probably composed around 1595:

> This England never did, nor never shall
> Lie at the proud foot of a conqueror
> But when it first did help to wound itself.
> Now these her princes are come home again
> [After King John's death ended the rebellions]
> Come the three corners of the world in arms
> And we shall shock them. Nought shall make us rue
> If England to itself do rest but true.
>
> *King John*, Act 5 Sc.7, 112–18

By the time that Shakespeare was writing his Histories in the 1590s, the Wars of the Roses, of which he wrote so much, belonged to a different age.

References

(Where early English writings other than Shakespeare are quoted in the text, the spelling has been modernized.)

Allmand, C. T. The Lancastrian land settlement in Normandy, 1417–50. In *The economic history review* (second series). **21**, pp.461–79, 1968.

Armstrong, C. A. J. (ed.) *Dominic Mancini, The usurpation of Richard III* (2nd edn). Oxford: Oxford University Press, 1969. (paperback) Gloucester: Alan Sutton, 1984.

Bennett, M. J. *Community, class and careerism: Cheshire and Lancashire society in the age of Sir Gawain and the Green Knight.* Cambridge: Cambridge University Press, 1983.

Buck, G. *The history of the life and reigne of Richard III.* London, 1646.

Byrne, M. StC. (ed.) *The Lisle Letters.* Chicago, Illinois: University of Chicago Press, 1981. Abridged edition: London: Secker and Warburg, 1983.

Campbell, L. B. (ed.) *The mirror for magistrates.* Cambridge: Cambridge University Press, 1938.

Campbell, L. B. *Shakespeare's "histories": mirrors of Elizabethan policy.* London: Methuen, 1964.

Carpenter, C. *Locality and polity: a study of Warwickshire landed society, 1401–1499.* Cambridge: Cambridge University Press, 1992.

Chrimes, S. B. and A. L. Brown (eds) *Select documents of English constitutional history 1307–1485.* London: Adam & Charles Black, 1961.

Clarke, M. V. *Fourteenth Century Studies.* Oxford: Clarendon Press, 1937.

Davies, J. S. (ed.) *An English chronicle of the reigns of Richard II, Henry IV, Henry V, and Henry VI.* London: Camden Society, Old Series, **64**, 1856.

Davis, N. (ed.) *Paston letters and papers of the fifteenth century* [2 parts]. Oxford: Clarendon Press, 1971–6.

Dockray, K. (ed.) *Three chronicles of the reign of Edward IV, with an introduction by Keith Dockray.* Gloucester: Alan Sutton, 1988.

Dunham, W. H. jr. *Lord Hasting's indentured retainers 1461–1483*. New Haven: Transactions of the Connecticut Academy of Arts and Sciences, 39, 1955.

Ellis, H. (ed.) *Three books of Polydore Vergil's English history*. London: Camden Society Old Series 29, 1844.

Fryde, N. *The tyranny and fall of Edward II 1321–1326*. Cambridge: Cambridge University Press, 1979.

Gairdner, J. *The life and reign of Richard III*. Cambridge: Cambridge University Press, 1898.

Gairdner, J. (ed.) *The Paston letters* [Library Edition, 6 vols], 1904. Microprint edition [1 vol.], Gloucester: Alan Sutton, 1983.

Gransden, A. *Historical writing in England ii: c.1307 to the early sixteenth century*. London: Routledge and Kegan Paul, 1982.

Griffiths, R. A. *The Reign of King Henry VI: the exercise of royal authority 1422–1461*. London: Ernest Benn, 1981.

Gunn, S. J. *Early Tudor government 1485–1558*. London: Macmillan, 1995.

Hall, E. *The union of the two noble and illustre famelies of Lancastre and Yorke*. London: R. Grafton, 1550. Reproduced by Scolar Press, 1970; there is also an edition by R. Grafton, 1548.

Halstead, C. A. *Richard III as Duke of Gloucester and King of England* [2 vols]. London: 1844.

Harriss, G. L. *King, parliament and public finance in Medieval England to 1369*. Oxford: Clarendon Press, 1975.

Harriss, G. L. *Henry V: The practice of kingship*. Oxford: Oxford University Press, 1985.

Harvey, I. M. W. *Jack Cade's rebellion of 1450*. Oxford: Clarendon Press, 1991.

Holinshed, R. *The chronicles of England, Scotlande and Irelande* [3 vols]. London, 1577.

Horrox, Rosemary *Richard III: a study of service*. Cambridge: Cambridge University Press, 1989.

Hoskins, W. G. *The age of plunder: King Henry's England 1500–1547*. London and New York: Longmans, 1976.

Kingsford, C. L. *Prejudice and promise in fifteenth century England*. Oxford: Clarendon Press, 1925.

McFarlane, K. B. *England in the fifteenth century*. London: Hambledon Press, 1981.

Maddicott. J. R. Magna Carta and the local community 1215–1259. *Past and present* 102, pp. 25–65, 1984.

Plummer. C. (ed.) *The governance of England by Sir John Fortescue kt*. London: Oxford University Press, 1885.

Pronay, N. and J. Cox, *The Crowland Chronicle continuations: 1459–1486.* London: Richard III and Yorkist History Trust, 1986.

Riley, H. T. (trans.) *Ingulph's chronicle of the Abbey of Croyland with the continuations by Peter of Blois and anonymous writers.* London: Bohn, 1854.

Ross, C. *Edward IV.* London: Eyre Methuen, 1974 [references are to the paperback edition of 1983].

Ross, C. *Richard III.* London: Eyre Methuen, 1981.

Saul, N. *Knights and esquires: the Gloucestershire gentry in the fourteenth century.* Oxford: Clarendon Press, 1981.

Starkey, D. et al. *The English court: from the wars of the roses to the civil war.* Harlow, England: Longman, 1987.

Stubbs, W. *The constitutional history of England* [3 vols]. Oxford: Clarendon Press, 1874.

Sylvester, R. S. (ed.) *The history of King Richard III* [vol. 2 of *The complete works of St. Thomas More.* New Haven, Connecticut: Yale University Press, 1963.

Thorpe, L. (trans.) *Geoffrey of Monmouth: the history of the kings of Britain.* Harmondsworth: Penguin, 1966.

Vergil, P. *Polydori Vergili Urbinatis Anglicae Historiae Libri XXVI.* Basle: J. Bebelium, 1534.

Walpole, H. Historic doubts on the life and reign of King Richard the third. London, 1768.

Wolffe, B. *Henry VI.* London: Eyre Methuen, 1981 [references are to the paperback edition of 1983].

Wright, S. M. *The Derbyshire gentry in the fifteenth century.* Chesterfield: Derbyshire Record Society, 8, 1983.

Further Reading

The References give details of the works I have cited in the text; but these are not always the most useful for those who want to go on to a fuller study of the period.

For a more detailed narrative than is possible here, the best guide is in the series of biographies in the *English monarchs* series: Wolffe, B. *Henry VI*. First published 1981; paperback, London: Methuen, 1983; Ross, C. *Edward IV*. First published 1974; paperback, London: Methuen, 1983; and Ross, C. *Richard III*. First published 1981; paperback, London: Methuen, 1988. There is also a larger work: Griffiths, R. A. *The reign of Henry VI: the exercise of royal authority 1422–1461*. London: Ernest Benn, 1981. There is a biography of George Duke of Clarence: Hicks, M. A. *False, fleeting, perjur'd Clarence*. Gloucester: Alan Sutton, 1980; and of the Duke of York: Johnson, P. A. *Duke Richard of York 1411–1460*. Oxford, Clarendon Press, 1988.

Particularly helpful specialized works are: Storey, R. L. *The end of the house of Lancaster*. First published 1966; paperback, Gloucester: Alan Sutton, 1986; and Horrox, R. *Richard III: a study of service*. Cambridge, Cambridge University Press, 1989. K. B. McFarlane's seminal essay on The Wars of the Roses was originally published in *The proceedings of the British Academy* 50, pp. 87–119, 1964; and is reprinted in McFarlane, K. B. *England in the Fifteenth Century*. London: Hambledon Press, 1981, pp. 231–67.

Manageable texts of the principal sources are to be found in Pronay, N. & J. Cox (eds) *The Crowland chronicle continuations, 1459–1486*. London: Richard III and Yorkist History Trust, 1986;

Dockray, Keith (ed.) *Three chronicles of the reign of Edward IV*. Gloucester: Alan Sutton, 1988; Armstrong, C. A. J. (ed.) *Dominic Mancini, the usurpation of Richard III* first published 1936; 2nd edn 1969; paperback, Gloucester: Alan Sutton, 1984. The most convenient edition of the Paston Letters is the reprint of James Gairdner's Library edition of 1904, as *The Paston letters edited by James Gairdner*. Gloucester: Alan Sutton, 1983. There is also a more recent edition, better edited but inconveniently arranged according to the Paston authors and recipients of the letters, in Davis, N. (ed.) *Paston letters and papers of the fifteenth century* [2 parts]. Oxford: Clarendon Press, 1971–76. There is a very useful brief collection of texts and comments on Richard III in Dockray, K. *Richard III: a reader in history*. Gloucester: Alan Sutton, 1988.

The most convenient guide to the "Tudor myth" is still Lily B. Campbell. *Shakespeare's "histories"*. London: Methuen, 1964. Shakespeare's version of the fifteenth century can be read in the series of plays, *Richard II*; *Henry IV, parts 1 and 2*; *Henry V*; *Henry VI, parts 1, 2 and 3*, and *Richard III*.

Index